Catfish Solution

The Power of Positive Poking

Nicholas Johnson

Also by Nicholas Johnson . . .

Columns of Democracy (Lulu Press, 2018)

Test Pattern for Living (3rd edition, Lulu Press, 2013)

How to Talk Back to Your Television Set (3rd and 4th editions, Lulu Press and Amazon Kindle, 2013)

From DC to Iowa: 2012 (Lulu Press, 2012)

Predicting Our Future Cyberlife: 1970-2040 (Lulu Press, 2012)

What Do You Mean and How Do You Know: An Antidote for the Language That Does Our Thinking for Us (Lulu Press, 2009)

Virtualosity: Eight Students in Search of Cyberlaw (Lulu Press, 2009)

Are We There Yet? Reflections on Politics in America (Lulu Press, 2008)

Your Second Priority: A Former FCC Commissioner Speaks Out (Lulu Press, 2008)

Catfish Solution

The Power of Positive Poking

Nicholas Johnson

Lulu Press
Morrisville, North Carolina
May 2019

ISBN: 978-0-359-61313-7

With thanks to:

Mary Vasey – my wife, my life, my love – and retired English teacher; any errors are the result of not following her advice.

Gregory Johnson – AboutGregJohnson.com – my son and tech guru, without whose creativity and skills this book would have had neither covers nor formatting.

Mary Ann Tsucalas, for reading and proof reading an earlier version of this book and her dedication and professional assistance throughout the author's years at MARAD and the FCC.

My parents, teachers, mentors, friends, co-workers, support staff, interns, enemies, critics, supporters, fans, elected and appointed officials, journalists, students and the others who made possible the first 40 years of the personal and professional life reflected in these pages.

See also Acknowledgements and Cover Photo Credits sections.

Table of Contents

Introduction

This book, first dusted off and published in 2019, was written in 1974 following my term as commissioner at the Federal Communications Commission, 1966-1973. For journalists, lawyers, business persons, sociologists, law professors, or anyone else desiring an inside view of the workings of government, here are some insights. For historians and those working within or studying the communications industries and FCC, this is a report of some turbulent years, with clues of how things got to where they are today. For those despairing of the current state of our government and democracy, searching for solutions, much of the content is as relevant today as when written, including suggestions for citizen-driven reform.

President Ronald Reagan, in his 1981 Inaugural Address famously said, "In this present crisis, government is not the solution to our problem; government is the problem." Similar comments disparaging government are legion. Some of what is in this book might appear to be among them. Therefore, clarification is in order:

(1) It is my best guess that from 1933 through 1980 many-to-most of those choosing to work in government agencies were motivated by genuine desire to provide public service and see government promote Americans' "life, liberty and the pursuit of happiness," to borrow from the Declaration of Independence.

1

(2) Many of the presidential appointees and civil servants I've come to know are among the most able, bright, committed, ethical, and hardworking individuals I've ever met. That goes for the occasional business person as well.

(3) To the extent small to serious corruption exits, sometimes called "industry capture" of regulatory agencies, it comes at least as much or more from pressure applied by industry and elected officials as from within the agency.

(4) Since the 1980s, and certainly since 2017, it has been my impression (for which I neither have nor offer data) that a larger percentage of appointees and those accepting government employment are motivated by partisan ends and future private sector employment.

(5) As for solutions to corporate overreach, my view is "it depends." If a community has a half-dozen grocery stores, aside from health and price-fixing concerns there is little need for a Grocery Store Regulatory Commission. The marketplace, with antitrust enforcement as needed, is sometimes better able to serve the public interest than an industry more heavily regulated by a government agency. Similarly, public ownership and operation, often using private sector contractors, may be a better model than private ownership for national defense, roads and bridges, local and national parks, public education and libraries, courts and prisons – among other functions, services and facilities.

There have been some modest editorial revisions within the 1974 text. But there has been no effort to update. To do so would produce a very different book and compromise the integrity of this snapshot in time.

These are the near-contemporaneous thoughts of a young, outspoken government official about a Washington, D.C., of the 1960s and 1970s. References to dates (e.g., "last year"), dollar amounts (e.g., 2019 values are about six times those in 1970), persons (and their titles), places and events should be read and understood in that context.

– Nicholas Johnson, May 2019.

# # #

Introduction (1974)

This book started out to be a chronicle of my years as an FCC commissioner (1966-1973). It has now become much more. It includes a reference to Twentieth-Century second and third-generation immigrants, and the childhood that started me down the road to the FCC. It tries to answer why a Supreme Court Justice from Alabama, who chose his law clerks from the South, would pick an Iowa boy as his law clerk. Why did a U.S. president choose someone in his twenties, from a landlocked state, whose only shipping experience involved an inability to operate a canoe safely, to administer the nation's shipping and ship building programs? It includes some insights into our legal system and law schools from the perspectives of a student, professor and practitioner. What is the process I discovered that explains how and why Washington forces produce the congressional and administrative decisions they do? What is the role of mass media in our democracy, and why is the FCC not doing more to improve it?

The stories could be interesting and instructive from several perspectives. For purposes of this Introduction, we'll stick with the FCC.

At a time of concern about our nation's economy – a simultaneous recession and inflation – it's useful to know about the impact of federal independent regulatory commissions upon that economy. For example, the FCC is supposed to regulate the American Telephone and Telegraph Company – a corporation with about $50 billion in assets, an annual budget of about $20 billion and 800,000 employees. A single rate increase case before the Commission resulted in additional payments by American consumers of some $1.3 billion a year. According to the FCC trial staff, the FCC Administrative Law Judge, and my own staff it was an increase totally unjustified by the record before the Commission.

Many of the industries the FCC regulates have a multi-billion-dollar impact upon our economy – the broadcasting industry, emerging cable television industry, communications satellites both international and domestic, offshore cables, private microwave networks, computer interconnection systems, and mobile radios (*e.g.*, radio amateurs, taxicabs and police cars).

The lessons that can be learned from the FCC's mishandling of its segment of our economy may be applicable with only minor variations to the Civil Aeronautics Board's regulation of airlines, Federal

Power Commission's regulation of natural gas and electric utilities, and Interstate Commerce Commission's regulation of railroads and trucking companies. Hopefully the book will be of use to businessmen, professors and students of economics, as well as other citizens curious to know more about the malfunctioning of our economy.

The FCC also represents a microcosm of the political process. Most of what the federal government does that matters isn't done on the floor of the House of Representatives, Senate or in the president's Oval Office. The business is transacted in the dingy gray offices and corridors of aging temporary buildings, the solid mausoleums built during President Franklin Roosevelt's day, or the eight-story plastic-and-glass buildings leased by the government from speculators in Washington real estate.

The political process that matters does not involve one of the three branches of government, but rather what might better be called subgovernments. How this political process works, who makes up the subgovernments, and how they serve the interests of big business is another theme of this book. It is a subject which has not received the attention it should from professors and students of economics, law and political science – or from the political pundits and journalists who provide the American people with much of their understanding of the modern-day political process.

There is also the process of decision making, the procedures used by government agencies to formulate significant national policy. Credibility gaps and cynicism notwithstanding, there is still a presumption abroad that governmental agencies are collections of expertise. Brilliant minds and computers coupled with masses of data are engaged in some rational process of policy formulation. What goes on in fact is far from that ideal. There may be those in the fields of public administration and business management who will find some insight here.

Finally, there is what many would assume to be the most obvious subject – communications policy. Communications touches every facet of our lives. The telephone brought as much social, political and economic revolution as did the automobile in an earlier age and television during the last twenty years. The emphasis of the Federal Communications Commission is almost exclusively on the engineering and legal aspects of communications policy, with a newfound halting interest in economic analysis. Yet the family, social, psychological, economic and political impact of its decisions are almost wholly ignored. Students of communications will perhaps find here a fuller understanding of why our communications policies serve the ends they do.

Throughout it all, I try to retain a sense of the humor and human dynamics that make up an institution like the Federal Communications Commission. My underlying feelings toward my colleagues and fellow workers are far more those of compassion than of contempt. But throughout my seven-and-a-half years, I found it most conducive to my own sanity to approach the institution and the daily routine like a novelist or anthropologist as well as a serious participant. That perspective may have seeped through some of this material as well.

By the end of the book you will have encountered some suggestions for improvement, and probably have a better sense of why so many of my FCC opinions ended up as dissents.

8 – Catfish Solution

Chapter One
Educating a Dissenter: The Early Years

It Is difficult to separate my experience, insights and memories of the Federal Communications Commission from my own background and personality – and I do not try. There are no known deliberate misrepresentations in this book, but neither can anyone, including this author, guarantee the truth of recollections. Memories evolve with time and their retelling. Others could write about these seven and a half years (1966-1973); some already have. Their recollections and opinions may differ from mine.

It is only fair to provide a brief sketch of the upbringing, experiences and perspective that accompanied me when arriving at the Federal Communications Commission on July 1, 1966.

If you disagree, and would rather skip this chapter, you might want to start with chapters two or three.

If you'd like to know more, read on.

Students in high school, college, law school, and teachers engaged in career counseling may find it useful to read about the forces that moved the author to government service. During informal question and answer sessions with students they often ask about the path to, as they put it, "get into government."

Secondly, any piece of writing – including court opinions and newspaper stories – is in part about the author as well as the subject at hand. The more you know about an author the more your comprehension and ability to challenge his or her assertions is enhanced.

Finally, this book is an unabashed personal account of what I did, said and thought as an FCC Commissioner. It makes no pretense of being an unbiased, academic analysis. It is almost impossible to understand what any individual did from age 31 to 39 without some notion of what happened during the prior 30 years. In any event, here are selections from my first three decades.

My life has involved a heavy measure of the academic – a word intentionally used to connote both its pejorative and positive qualities.

I was literally born on a university campus – the University of Iowa Hospital – in Iowa City, Iowa, during the fall of 1934. Both my parents grew up as farm kids, children of immigrants; she, Edna Bockwoldt, from northwest Iowa, he, Wendell Johnson, from northeast Kansas. Both came to Iowa City about the same time and were University of Iowa graduates. My father created and directed at that University one of the world's first and principal center for research in speech pathology (stuttering and related speech and hearing handicaps). He attended Alfred Korzybski's lectures on general semantics (the role of language in human behavior, as distinguished from a "semantics" of defining words). Dad wrote *People in Quandaries* and helped launch the

International Society for General Semantics and its journal, *ETC*, with Drs. S. I. Hayakawa, Anatol Rapoport and Irving J. Lee. I was brought up with general semantics and it helped to shape my broad, social-impact understanding of communications while at the FCC.

A strong undercurrent of humanist values came from my parents, their friends, school, Unitarian Church, and reading. Those values remain to this day.

Iowa City was an intellectually stimulating small town during 1934 to 1952 and remains so today. It is occasionally characterized as "the Athens of the Midwest," and still brags of more poetry and novels per person than any city of comparable size in the United States, along with similar Chamber of Commerce and University claims.

The town was small enough even as a child you, as small-town folks say, "knew everybody." It seemed to me at the time there was almost total blindness to socio-economic status, racial or religious differences. The fellow who sold popcorn and soft drinks at the college ballgames, and the *Iowa City Press-Citizen* outside Racine's Cigar Store, was as well-known a personality as the president of the bank across the street, football coach or University president.

The Iowa Child Welfare Research Station was one of the first to study so-called "normal children." Notwithstanding that entry requirement, I was admitted to the two-year-old, three-year-old and four-year-old groups. At age five I moved down the street to a kindergarten in the University's experimental schools, the first of 13 years in a building with an elementary and high school until graduation in 1952. Twenty years later I was asked to deliver the last commencement address before the University closed the schools ("The Last Commencement Address: The U High Idea," June 1, 1972).

Rather than the expensive, elite, private school one might imagine, a legal fluke made U High even more egalitarian than Iowa City's public schools. Schools were provided by townships. The townships around Iowa City each had so few students they could not afford high schools. By law, townships without high schools had to send their students, and pay their tuition, to school districts that did. Because U High charged lower tuition than Iowa City's high school, City High, U High's student body was predominantly farm and small-town kids along with those of us raised in professors' homes. They were not only fully competitive academically in high school and college, they also enabled the rest of us to maintain some measure of respectability athletically in Eastern Iowa Hawkeye Conference basketball, football and track.

Our teachers were University professors with a commitment and sense of excitement about educational process that transferred to us. In addition to our being their students, we were the subjects, the guinea pigs, for their creation, testing and revision of the nationally accepted Iowa Tests of Educational Development, as well as other research. Only later, when my children were educated in what were said to be good public schools, did it become obvious how exceptional the University of Iowa Elementary and High School education had been. There are few schools approaching their teaching and research quality today and the nation is the poorer for that.

We were encouraged to develop a sense of our own individuality and worth (what a theologian might characterize as "divine spark") in an atmosphere in which such growth was not only tolerated but positively encouraged. Of course, critics might use words like "permissive" and "lack of discipline," but we didn't do crazy stuff and neither individuals nor physical property suffered discernable damage.

Once trained to challenge teachers, challenging the notions of fellow FCC commissioners with dissenting opinions came naturally. The notion that it is possible, even sometimes commendable, to dissent was enhanced with early knowledge of the dissents of Justices Hugo Black, Louis Brandeis, Benjamin Cardozo, William Douglas, Oliver Wendell Holmes and others. To do so as a member of a multi-person administrative agency was illustrated for me by the dissents of Federal Trade Commission Commissioner Philip Elman (1961-1970) while I was Maritime Administrator. Justice Black was a special hero with his dissents, though as a high school student the prospect of my someday serving as his law clerk did not even appear in dreams.

U-High's courses would sometimes involve writing our own textbooks, as in geometry. Most teachers believed our love of learning, and skill with methods of learning, was more important than memorization of facts. Whether in spite of their approach or because of it, we seemed regularly to better the state-wide test scores of our peers in other schools.

Out of this early experience came a respect for the intellectual and rational process as an approach, if not the only approach, to problem solving and public policy. We also developed a commitment to public purpose and public service – whether by a research psychologist or an elected public official. It was unthinkable even to contemplate private profit from public business, particularly if it would involve even the slightest compromise of the public interest.

My own academic interests tended to focus on the social sciences, government, law and politics. The first reported indication of a commitment to popular representation and social change came in the fourth grade. We students organized what may have been one of the early student sit-ins – for this occasion in our grade school principal's office. Our demand was for an elementary school student council. That our request was granted was considered a great victory. In retrospect, Principal Herbert F. Spitzer was probably thrilled beyond words with this evidence of student initiative and would only have wondered why we waited so long with our demand.

During junior high I worked as a janitor and night watchman for the Iowa-Illinois Gas and Electric Company. After cleaning and waxing floors, it was my responsibility to open the community meeting room for local civic groups and lock up when they left.

My parents had given me a copy of *The Autobiography of Lincoln Steffens*, and I used the long evenings reading what seemed an incredibly lengthy volume. I was turned on by Steffens' challenge to communities around the turn of the century. He claimed he could find corruption in any American community within a couple weeks.

Iowa City struck me as the perfect place to test his thesis. Peacefully nestled along the Iowa River, peopled by intelligentsia and upstanding merchants, it was simply unthinkable Steffens could find corruption in Iowa City.

Once I learned Lincoln Steffens obtained much of his information from waitresses and taxi drivers I began looking for and interviewing waitresses and taxi drivers. Many were willing to share what they knew.

Within three days they told me of charges that bribery had occurred with purchases of trucks and parking meters. The most horrifying discovery was a plan to locate the City's swimming pool on farmland seven miles from town rather than the City Park.

Investigation revealed a member of the City Council had an interest in that land. A classmate and friend of mine, Dick DeGowin, arranged our first introduction to city government and politics. His mother, president of the local League of Women Voters, explained what was then Iowa City's ward system for council members. We began circulating a petition throughout the ward of the councilman who owned the land.

We then attended a City Council meeting and placed the petition on the bench in front of that council member, while presenting as persuasive a speech as we could muster. Ever after we've had a little extra pride when we drive by the pool in Iowa City's Park.

My mother's father, Mox Bockwoldt, arrived in America on his own in 1890 as a 15-year-old speaking no English. After a course in double-entry bookkeeping in Davenport he made his way to a lifetime of farming and business in northwest Iowa. He served in the Iowa House of Representatives for sixteen years and once gave me a tour of the House Chamber where I was permitted to sit in his seat. I was very proud and fond of him. When he presented me a gift of the *1939 Code of Iowa* I not only read it from cover to cover (with some fast skimming through the building code) but was inspired by it to use precious paper-route money to buy a copy of the *1936 Municipal Code of Iowa City*.

My reading of Iowa City's *Code* led to my first successful court case.

The first fellow in my class with a driver's license was Lou Maher. Lou and I would occasionally shop for electronics equipment. We never bought any as I recall, but we did spend time looking. One day we emerged from a World War II war surplus store to discover Lou's car, parked in the alley, had a parking ticket under the windshield wiper. We could scarcely afford gasoline, and certainly couldn't pay parking tickets.

I agreed to be Lou's lawyer, prepared myself on the local law of alley parking, and argued our case before the local justice of the peace. Relying on the loading zone provisions of the *Code*, which authorized alley parking for those loading merchandise, I created and argued a doctrine of constructive loading. Surely the drafters of the authorized alley-parking exception must have intended to include the *possibility* of loading within the exemption for loading. After all, no one can know when parking in an alley whether the store will have, and they will be loading, that which they have come to purchase. Lou was found innocent, although admonished not to do it again.

This left me a little perplexed at the time: if I was correct, and we had done no wrong, why should we not do it again? If, on the other hand, there was no doctrine of constructive loading, shouldn't we have been fined? It was only years later that I became aware of the fact that the Justice of the Peace, Emil Trot, was also a graduate of University High School and was undoubtedly approaching our behavior from much the same perspective as my elementary school principal received our demand for a student council.

During junior high Dick, other of our young friends and I formed what we called the Junior Bureau of Investigation. We collected old wanted posters from the Postmaster, Sheriff, and Chief of Police. After I wrote a text for the group on fingerprint classification we used the fingerprints on the posters for training exercises. We wrote FBI Director J. Edgar

Hoover of our willingness to provide local assistance to his organization. Although he sent us literature and encouragement, he kindly explained why we could not be a Johnson County Chapter of the Federal Bureau of Investigation. (Of the six of us, three ended up as medical school professors, two as law professors, and one as a Ph.D. chemistry professor.)

This activity led to what all of us believed to be my first encounter with the FCC.

A University of Iowa criminology professor, Richard Holcomb, administered an annual Iowa Peace Officers Short Course for state and local law enforcement officers which he invited us to attend. That was where we learned of the importance of communications to police work, and Mr. Holcomb provided us some catalogs from radio equipment suppliers.

Since none of us had either a police car or the money to acquire radio equipment we bought a ten-in-one kit from Allied Radio in Chicago for thirteen dollars. The catalog informed us that with this kit we would be able to build from among the ten choices a phono oscillator. This device was intended to enable the utilization of an AM radio receiver to play music, from a phonograph without an amplifier, through the radio's amplifier and speaker.

To broadcast from the phonograph to the radio an antenna was attached to the phono oscillator. The instructions warned that one should never use more than a 25-foot antenna. This was exactly the wrong thing to advise junior high school boys. We promptly climbed out the attic window onto the roof of my parents' home and began stringing up 500 feet of braided copper wire.

Although the voice transmission would only broadcast on unused frequencies we discovered when we broadcast in Morse code the signal could be received on a car radio parked directly under the transmitter of the 5,000-kilowatt local radio station, WSUI. Scarcely had our experiment concluded when one of our members, Howard Berg, reported from Iowa City's east side that he had seen an FCC monitoring truck. We never knew the truth of that report, but I always suspected that the time it took us to turn that transmitter back into a ten-in-one kit radio receiver would have set a record.

During the Second World War Iowa City was the location for a U.S. Navy pre-flight training school. We learned how to communicate with semaphore flags, ran the obstacle course, rooted for their Seahawks' ball teams, and went on their hikes. We were as welcomed by them as we were by the University professors whose laboratories we wandered through as if they were our playrooms. (One of our friends, Jerry Holland, became acquainted with John Glenn at that time and was later rewarded with appointment to Annapolis, where he now teaches, having completed a tour as captain of a submarine.)

I also attended a Navy course in Morse Code and, after our near run-in with the FCC, constructed a telegraph service between my house and that of neighbor Willie Weber. The use of wire required pounding nails through the roof of Willie's house, the leaks from which his mother, Martha, still remembers to this day. It also involved draping copper wire through the trees of a neighbor's yard which significantly weakened the signal. My mother suggested if we really wanted to talk to each other we might just use the telephone, but mothers never understand such things.

The high school was sufficiently small, maybe 200 or 300 students, that everyone necessarily participated in virtually every activity. There were three or four bands in which I played a variety of instruments while participating in all varsity sports, the full range of drama and speech activities, student council and several clubs. The debating team, which won state-wide championships, brought me to a serious consideration of public policy issues long before it otherwise would have happened, as well as providing some experience in analyzing and presenting issues in public speaking. We always had current events discussions in our social science classes exposing us to what was going on in the world. In my senior year John Haefner's course, "Readings in Social Studies," introduced us to Plato, Machiavelli, Marx, and the Utopians.

My interest in student politics evolved about the sophomore year in high school; I was elected president of the student council both my junior year (which was unprecedented at U High) and re-elected my senior year. Along the way I was also elected President of the Iowa Association of Student Councils and served for three years as the National

President of Hi-Y – the high school branch of the Young Men's Christian Association (YMCA).

The Hi-Y position carried with it the opportunity to represent the YMCA to the United Council of Churches (UCC) and its high school component, the United Christian Youth Movement (UCYM). The irony of a young Unitarian representing Hi-Y to an affiliate of a UCC that refused membership to the Unitarian Church was not lost on me. When I complained that a young men's organization really should have someone under the age of 65 on its board of directors, I was promptly appointed. That was to be my first experience as a minority group spokesperson. It also gave me my first contact with some of the country's top business leaders, and exposure to what I would subsequently come to know as systems analysis.

"What is the role of a Hi-Y in the 1950's?" I asked and discovered another lesson that was to serve me well in Washington 25 years later. When it comes to the fundamental issues – such as "what is our purpose and why are we bothering with this at all?" – not only does no one have the answers, the odds are no one has even asked the questions.

"Now that schools and city recreation departments are providing facilities formerly only provided by the Y should we reconsider our recreation facilities program?" I asked. "And where does the 'Christian' part come in? Is the dance my local Hi-Y puts on somehow more Christian than the dance sponsored by my high school Letterman's Club? It sounds like the same words and music to me." Years later somebody told me they were going to have a study of Hi-Y, but I don't think I was sent a copy, and I wouldn't bet major changes were made.

One of my first trips to Washington alone was for a YMCA Youth in Government program. I then presumed it must be about the most important thing going on in Washington, as we went from agency to agency for briefings and debates of public policy issues. As Maritime Administrator and FCC Commissioner I would meet with Washington study groups of high school and college students and try to recall the special feeling I had about my own experience when their age.

In a few years you will be responsible for the operation of the government. ... Inform yourselves.
– President Harry S. Truman, Remarks, White House, June 26, 1952

The chance to meet President Harry S. Truman would have been something special at any time. He struck us as friendly and natural, and genuinely interested in our following careers in government as he spoke of his earlier years of Kansas City court house politics.

Such programs do have their impact. A few years later when I had a chance to spend the summer in Washington, D.C., as a law student clerk at Covington & Burling, I snapped at it – while my University of Texas classmates chose summer jobs in Austin, Dallas, and Houston. I spent that summer plowing through thousands of pages of FCC opinions, trying to find a pattern to the award of TV licenses in comparative hearings. The only pattern involved newspaper ownership. Commissioners appointed as Republicans were often unconcerned about common ownership of papers and stations. Democratic Party appointees were more likely to consider it a demerit.

There was an opportunity in high school to participate as a student senator for a day or two in the State Capitol building in Des Moines. We debated and enacted legislation. Having been splattered with mud by semi-trucks I drafted, introduced, lobbied for, and succeeded in enacting a bill requiring trucks to be equipped with mud flaps. The idea caught on and ultimately was enacted by the real legislature. It was a proud experience to return to the chambers my grandfather had first shown me.

After graduating from high school, I married a grade school and high school classmate, Karen Chapman, and we went to the University of Texas in Austin together. We each held a couple part-time jobs apiece, had our first child, Julie, carried a full load of course work, managed our apartment house, and lived on $1200-to-$1300 a year. Karen earned a degree in education and began teaching. I majored in political science and then attended and graduated from the University of Texas Law School. We both made a deliberate choice to avoid student activities and use this time in our lives to concentrate on education though there were plenty of temptations to do otherwise.

We chose Texas both because it would have been a little awkward for both of us, if attending the University of Iowa, to have neighbors and long-time family friends as professors, and because I had a sinus condition for which Texas was believed to be the answer. It was.

But once there we found just being in Texas during the 1950's (1952-1958, plus a year in Houston) was an education for a couple of Iowa kids. Nationally these were the years of President Eisenhower, Senator Joseph McCarthy and the Silent Generation. Politically the state was divided between the Democrats who voted for Republican presidential candidates (conservative wing), and Democrats who voted for the Democratic presidential candidates (labor, liberal, loyalists). The oil and gas industry had considerable political power.

And yet in the middle of Texas, amongst the conservative-oil-McCarthy-racist population was a small cluster of Texans not unlike the people we'd known in Iowa City.

Yet there was a difference. The difference was that they were eking out an existence in a very hostile environment and were toughened by their guerilla lifestyle. Intellectual freedom was a prized possession they were willing to and had to fight for. Of course, there were those who would rather settle for a nice job with an oil company, and all the country club privileges thereto pertaining. But they could not avoid the realization they were making a choice. They could not unconsciously slide into that verdant pasture; they full well knew they'd chosen to switch rather than fight.

We had to picket to open a local movie theater to Blacks. The dormitories had to be integrated. The first Black had only recently been admitted to the Texas Law School by a U.S. Supreme Court decision (*Sweatt v. Painter*, 339 U.S. 629 (1950)). The first Black came onto UT's football fields during our years there. There were black and white drinking fountains and often rows of rest rooms – professionals, working class, public – all divided by Black and white as well as men and women.

Eleanor Roosevelt was forbidden to speak on campus. Willie Morris, the author of *North Toward Home*, had to risk his job as *Daily Texan* editor and challenge an official censor because the Regents had been angered by his daring to carry AP news items impliedly critical of the natural gas industry. The revered law school dean, Page Keeton, had to put his job on the line more than once as did various chancellors.

As a local precinct captain I began to see the relationship between political power and money. The abject poverty of Black East Austin stood in stark contrast to the palatial homes in the hills of white West Austin. When those in power forced others into a life of poverty, inadequate education and the poll tax, the result was only 10 percent of East Austin voted while 90 percent of West Austin did – thereby both legitimizing and perpetuating the inequity.

Central to the consciousness-raising process (for those of us who experienced it) was former *Daily*

Texan Editor Ronnie Dugger's *The Texas Observer* begun in 1954. It was one of the first and best of what ten years later were called underground newspapers. It spawned numerous first-class writers, including Bill Bramer, whose novel *The Gay Place* also describes the Austin and Texas of the 1950s of which Willie Morris wrote.

Although merely living in and being forced to the choices Texas offered in the 1950s was education enough, my course work was not incidental. Largely through former students and friends of my father and others at Iowa, I was able to make contacts in each department of the University of Texas that were willing to help me find the best of their colleagues.

Dr. Bill Wolfe was especially helpful. Dr. Bill Livingston helped steer me into political science. In any event, the result was that I had first-class professors for all my courses, from freshman English on. This gave me contact with good minds; men and women interested in education, ideas and excellence. It was as nearly a continuation of what University High School offered as one could find at a state university.

My junior year there was a coincidental combination of courses that had a collective impact upon me and would later influence my understanding of corporate domination of television. There was a cultural anthropology course taught by an iconoclastic Professor J. Gilbert McAllister, once described as "a Texas liberal confronting galloping McCarthyism and deep Texas conservatism." He had us read, among other things, Ruth Benedict's *Patterns of Culture.*

Dr. McDonald's course in Twentieth Century Political Thought introduced the class to Arthur Koestler's *Darkness at Noon* and George Orwell's *1984* (also assigned reading in two or three other courses). Dr. Robert R. Blake's social psychology course opened my eyes to some of the early experiments studying how an individual's behavior and observations could be altered by a group. A very colorful professor of agricultural economics, Dr. Montgomery, gave a series of lectures (having nothing to do with either agriculture or economics) attended by as many visitors as students. He was the one who introduced me to Thorstein Veblen's *The Theory of the Leisure Class*, which ultimately influenced my book, *Test Pattern for Living*. Moreover, this was followed during my law school years with the combined impact on the national consciousness of books such as Vance Packard's *Hidden Persuaders*, William H. Whyte's *The Organization Man* and C. Wright Mills' *The Power Elite*.

The combination of course work and political realities of Texas gave me a perspective that has proven useful over the years. America does have a class system. It was obvious to me walking a few blocks east or west from our Austin apartment. Wealth and power tend to reinforce each other. They are occasionally associated with oppression of individuals and ideas that stand in their way. They often practice excessive materialism. Texas gaudy is merely a comic caricature, a less hypocritical rendition of the tasteless greed of those for whom "more is better and too much is not enough."

From power and oppression can come bending of the human spirit, the twisting of ideas, values and lifestyle into forms that more smoothly serve the economic interests of those who control. To prevent this requires a massive effort at consciousness raising.

Those who seek to reform such a system – such as Dr. Martin Luther King and Senator Robert Kennedy – must be prepared to exhibit extraordinary courage in confronting those who have the power to bring them untold misery and even death.

I would later come to understand the role of television in this process.

Chapter Two
The Law: Training and Practice

After college the CIA wanted to interview me (never seriously considered it), did interview for the Foreign Service (U.S. State Department), avoided interviews with corporations, and ultimately decided to attend law school. This was not so much a perception of law as a rational path to a life of social reform as a way station; the all-purpose graduate program. Law school could provide relevant training for business, government service, teaching – as well as the practice of law. It would provide three more years to mull over decisions about a career.

Law school also appeared from a distance to offer rigorous training in analytical process. Once back in Austin, now in law school, I was not disappointed. Not all professors and students were equally gifted intellectually, but all at least seemed to be striving for excellence and tidiness of mind. Maybe I took it more seriously than other students, but probably not. We were reminded of Justice Oliver Wendell Holmes admonition, "The business of a law school is ... to teach law in the grand manner and to make great lawyers." [Remarks, Harvard College's 250th Anniversary, 1886.] Such an environment provided a felt obligation to develop one's knowledge and skills, as a medical student might feel, because of the professional responsibility, not to mention the grief one might forever carry at having inadequately protected another's fortune or life.

Law school had its impact in a variety of ways. The first-year spirit was sometimes akin to what I imagined in a Marine Corps boot camp. The efforts and skills were different from an undergraduate college education, success was guaranteed to no one, and long hours and hard work seemed the only possible response. Years later, *The Paper Chase* (1973), a movie about law school, reminded me of my own experiences. The analytical skills – dissecting court opinions and statutes, arguing from one line of cases to another – tend to be somewhat dehumanizing. Because of an occasional Judge Learned Hand or Justice Oliver Wendell Holmes opinion there is some regard for good writing, and torts law (injuries) has occasional flashes of humor and passion for the plaintiff. But property, procedure, bills and notes, and the rest of the standard curriculum are generally in a metaphysical world all their own – kind of like playing three-dimensional chess and trying to remember where all the pieces are. And except for a rare Fred Rodell (Yale law professor and author, *Woe Unto You Lawyers* (1939)) it is rare that anyone inside the legal establishment subjects the whole legal system to the ridicule occasionally deserved.

The law school curriculum puts a heavy emphasis upon the rights of property, the rich, and large corporations. This has changed markedly in the last twenty years with courses in poverty law, civil rights, and consumer protection. But that revolution was only beginning in the 1950s, and even today the orientation of the curriculum in most law schools has not changed that much. I was uncomfortable with this emphasis, but not openly rebellious.

The faculty was first rate, largely due to the efforts of Dean Page Keeton (my torts professor). I worked as a student assistant (the law school title was "quizmaster") for the prior Dean, C.T. McCormick, who was also my evidence and contracts professor. Another Dean (Northwestern University School of Law), Leon Green, offered a course he created titled "Injuries to Relations" I enjoyed. A brilliant and prolific young professor, Charles Alan Wright, taught my constitutional law class. He later came to be known to the legal profession for his work on the federal courts treatise, and to the public for his defense of Richard Nixon. Others – Gus Hodges, Corwin Johnson, Millard Ruud, George Stumberg, Jerre Williams, Bill Young – provided not only an understanding of their own specialized area of the law, but of legal ethics, professionalism and excellence.

The law review experience was harrowing but invaluable. It was probably my first time in nineteen years of schooling to be subjected to such rigorous training in writing and editing. A casenote of a couple pages in the *Texas Law Review* (a discussion of a current court decision) could take six weeks to research, and ten drafts to write and edit into something the editors would accept.

My classmates and I talked over our plans after graduation. There were long arguments about the relative merits of large and small firms – a subject about which we had neither experience nor expertise. Some wanted to represent criminals and injured plaintiffs. Most were content to practice corporate and securities law with Texas' largest firms or oil company legal departments. During the short time I was in law school we watched these firms' starting salaries go from $200 to $300 a month, and then $500. That kind of money was hard for law students to resist.

Charlie Wright (as he was colloquially known to students) told me about the option called a "judicial clerkship" and ultimately sold me on the idea. After Yale Law School he had clerked for Judge Charles E. Clark, U.S. Court of Appeals, 2nd Circuit. Clerking was then relatively new to University of Texas Law School faculty and students.

Law clerks are young, all-purpose personal assistants to state and federal judges, usually selected for one-year appointments. (They are unrelated to the position of clerk of the court, a relatively permanent administrative position serving judges, lawyers and the public, receiving and providing access to legal papers.)

Judges select their law clerks from among the top graduates of the nation's law schools each year. The one-year rotation has disadvantages for judges, who are constantly training new assistants, but it does insure judges will be rejuvenated and stimulated by law schools' latest ideas and graduates. Judges are expected to decide and write their court's opinions, but much of a judge's legal research can be handled by law-review-quality new law school graduates.

The law clerks probably have the better of the bargain. They are provided a year of paid post-graduate training in legal research, come to know rather intimately the workings of at least one judge's mind and decision-making process, meet members of the bar, and conclude their year ready to move into teaching, government or practice. (Nicholas Johnson, "What Do Law Clerks Do?" *Texas Bar Journal*, May 22, 1959.)

Judge John R. Brown was appointed to the United States Court of Appeals, 5th Circuit, in 1955 by President Dwight Eisenhower and expressed a willingness to take his clerks from the University of Texas Law School. Dean Keeton helped with Judge Brown's selection process, in return for which Judge Brown spoke at the law school's annual tax conference in Austin.

I was not the top student in my graduating class, but had done well, served as articles editor of the *Texas Law Review*, and not incidentally made the highest grade in Dean Keeton's torts class. Judge Brown agreed to an interview, and ultimately hired me.

In this country the federal court system exists side-by-side with our states' court systems. Each has trial courts and appellate courts. The federal district courts are the federal trial courts. The United States courts of appeals are, for most purposes, the final tribunal for any appeal from a federal district court. Appeals can be taken from a federal court of appeals to the U.S. Supreme Court on a petition for certiorari, but unlike the courts of appeals the Supreme Court can choose its cases. Out of thousands of requests, it may hear and issue opinions for fewer cases in a year than the FCC does in a week. Most will involve conflicts between decisions of U.S. courts of appeals, interpretation of the Constitution, federal statutes, or other significant principle of law.

The states are clustered into ten numbered regions, called circuits, each with its own federal court of appeals. At that time the Fifth Circuit included the Gulf Coast states, from west to east: Texas, Louisiana, Mississippi, Alabama, Georgia and Florida.

I had, and still have, a tremendous respect for Judge Brown (who at this time is Chief Judge of the Fifth Circuit). The contrast between his sense of humor and his position made him a spectacular public speaker and fun to work with. He had been an outstanding student at the University of Michigan Law School, had a good mind, and worked hard. Living and working in Houston, his previous specialty as a practicing lawyer was admiralty law, and he retained his interest in this salty and colorful bayou of the law.

He took a real interest in his clerks. Although the Judge lived in Houston, the Court's official location was New Orleans. It also sat in each of the states in the Fifth Circuit (except Mississippi). Because the Judge took his clerks with him, there was quite a bit of traveling and opportunity to experience America's segregated Southland.

One of my first experiences involved his insistence that I use a dictating machine – an alien technology previously unknown to me – to compose my briefing notes on the cases coming before the three-judge panels to which Judge Brown was assigned. My brief summaries of the facts and law were circulated to Judge Brown and the panel's other two judges. The thought of briefing real cases was exciting enough. The fact that judges rather than law professors were going to read and possibly be influenced by my analyses was intimidating. The prospect of dictating them without the chance for revision made it almost impossible for me to talk into the dictation machine at all.

While I retained my respect for the seriousness of the legal process, it was a valuable, liberating experience to internalize the realization that these cases are decided by humans. One wants to be responsible, fair and thorough. But having done that, nothing is gained by prolonged agonizing. It's better to pick up and read the briefs, think through the facts and law to a conclusion, dictate the memo, and move on to the next one.

One of my challenges in law school was trying to remember case names and holdings (the legal rule from the courts' decisions). Most legal training involves techniques of analysis, legal research, or spotting the issues. There's not as much focus on memorizing legal rules as students of biology or history might confront when memorizing their facts. But a memory is required and mine was relatively poor. What to do?

Ultimately, this approach evolved: read the court's statement of facts and both sides' arguments, figure out how it should be analyzed and decided, then read the court's analysis and decision. If the judge's analysis and decision is analogous to my own there is no need to remember that case. If those facts ever arose again, on a law school essay exam or later in practice, my instinct was equivalent to the law. (Of course, case holdings have to be researched and cited in any legal opinion or brief.) Only cases that did not square with my analysis and sense of justice would have to be memorized.

This instinct proved a good guide through two clerkships, teaching, practice, and jobs as Maritime Administrator and FCC commissioner. It was certainly reassuring whenever Judge Brown and his colleagues would end up agreeing with the analysis in my memo. (Even more so, of course, when a dissenting opinion of Judge Brown was supported by the Supreme Court.) The Fifth Circuit judges were almost all men for whom I had great respect (there were no women, as was common in those days): Chief Judge Joseph Chappell Hutcheson, Jr. (appointed 1931), Judge Richard T. Rives (1951), Judge Elbert Tuttle (1954), Judge John Robert Brown (1955), Judge Benjamin Franklin Cameron (1955), Judge Warren Leroy Jones (1955), and Judge John Minor Wisdom (1957). (Four of those seven lived well into their nineties.)

That year (1958-1959) the civil rights cases were already beginning, and the Fifth Circuit's record was one of which all Americans could be proud – especially considering the flaming crosses in judges' yards and other social pressures they confronted.

One of the men for whom I had greatest respect was U.S. Supreme Court Justice Hugo L. Black. My father spoke of him with admiration. I had read his opinions in government classes and law school and had long admired his tough insistence upon the basic provisions of the Constitution, his willingness to dissent, and his humanism. Each of the Justices has a responsibility for a circuit, and Justice Black's circuit was the Fifth – which contained his home state of Alabama.

Although Justice Black was getting one hundred or more applications from outstanding young lawyers for his clerkship positions (justices then had two), I decided to try for it. Judge Brown wrote a nice letter for me and so did Judge Rives – who was from Alabama and probably the closest to Justice Black.

The interview with Justice Black was really honor enough. That marble monument called the Supreme Court is one of the most beautiful and awesome buildings in Washington. When it opened one justice is said to have refused to work there on grounds the only appropriate way to arrive would be on the back of a large white elephant.

My first day, when my wife, Karen, drove north on First Street, pulled up and parked in front of the Court to let me out, our six-year-old daughter, Julie, responded much like that justice. She took one look at the building, turned to me with a look of incredulity and asked, "Daddy, do you work in *there*?" Thereafter my co-clerk, Jack McNulty, and I usually traded off driving each other to work.

John

The courtroom itself is one of the grandest rooms in the country. But for a young law school graduate to be escorted by a guard past the black wrought iron gates, down a long, high-ceilinged marble corridor to an appointment with Justice Black in the inner sanctum of the building was a real thrill.

As it turned out, he hired me, and I would regularly report to work there each day. But I never forgot the excitement of that first meeting, nor did constant exposure ever erode my real respect for Justice Black (known to his law clerks as "the Judge"), the building, and the legal system it symbolizes.

Much of my subsequent difficulty at the FCC is probably traceable to my experience at the Supreme Court. The Supreme Court experience gave me a benchmark by which to judge the performance of other court-like institutions, a benchmark by which the FCC sometimes becomes a laughing-stock. The standards to which the Court holds itself, while necessary and commendable, are unrealistic for most institutions. It's unfair to hold the FCC to the same standards as the Court in all cases. For starters, the FCC issues more opinions in an average week than the Supreme Court issues in a year. But it's not unfair when the Supreme Court's example is both applicable and attainable.

The justices read the lawyers' briefs, attend the oral argument, discuss the case in closed conference and vote on the outcome. The chief justice designates the justice to write the majority opinion. It is written, circulated among, and certainly carefully read by the others. If the author and eight more sign on it is a unanimous opinion. If a majority sign on, those disagreeing can write concurring or dissenting opinions. Occasionally a separate opinion is sufficiently persuasive to change other justices' votes. Justices write their own opinions. And to the extent their clerks offer research or debate the merits of a case with their justice, the Court has the assistance of a couple of the nation's ablest law school graduates.

At the FCC, by contrast, aside from my dissents it was somewhere between rare and never that a commissioner would author either a Commission ruling or separate opinion. Opinions are prepared by the staff of the relevant bureau (*e.g.,* Broadcast Bureau, Common Carrier Bureau), approved by the bureau chief, and put on the Commission's Wednesday agenda. Indeed, given the complexity and length of many of the opinions it's unlikely they were even closely read and comprehended by all commissioners if they were read at all.

There was little if any contact between Supreme Court justices and practicing lawyers. For a justice to meet with a lawyer about his or her pending case was unthinkable. There were few phone calls or visitors of any sort. Having experienced the standards of the Supreme Court it was difficult to avoid drawing contrasts with the FCC and encouraging my Commission colleagues to do a little better where their roles are similar.

Things are different at the FCC, and understandably so. The FCC is not just a court, hearing appeals from decisions of its staff and hearing examiners (the regulatory commissions' trial judges, now called administrative law judges). It is also a legislative body, with the power to enact regulations said to have "the force and effect of law," using a legislative process during which appropriate direct contact between legislators and interested parties may be acceptable.

The Supreme Court deals with few lawyers or clientele on a regular basis (except the government's lawyer, the Solicitor General in the Justice Department). The FCC sees almost no one other than its regular customers (members of the Federal Communications Bar Association, major corporations' executives and lobbyists), all of whom are well known and often former colleagues and social friends of the commissioners and staff.

Of course, it's more difficult for commissioners and staff to maintain a professional distance from their small, specialized clientele than it is for the Supreme Court justices to keep a distance from the entire nation's bar membership. But greater efforts could be made to police commissioners' social and other private contacts with industry representatives.

At the Maritime Administration a log was kept of every person entering the Office of Ship Construction. If every FCC commissioner's office and bureau at the FCC was required to keep a public list of the names and affiliations of individuals telephoning or visiting the agency some of the grosser abuses would be reduced.

There is a measure of insecurity and anti-intellectualism within the Commission that discourages the use of able independent minds. There is also a lack of appreciation for the drawing power the Commission could have. My hiring practices followed the courts' law clerk model: high quality young lawyers for one-year terms. Other commissioners could do likewise. Individuals with no interest in an FCC career might be willing to consider a one-year assignment in a commissioner's office. Scientists, systems analysts, economists and other social scientists who wouldn't think of accepting civil service status might be willing to serve on advisory committees or take phone calls. I never had difficulty drawing upon America's best minds.

To be fair, it's not the staff's fault that there is likely to be more research, tight reasoning and intellectual content in an opinion that Supreme Court justices and their clerks have leisurely labored over for a month or more than one a low-level FCC civil servant has worked on for a day while attending meetings, handling phone calls, and answering congressional correspondence.

But the failure to be analytical and precise, to cite serious research, books, articles, and court opinions, is motivated in part by the staff's awareness that commissioners don't want to make ringing declarations of principle that might bind their flexibility in future cases. Some of the Commission's irrational opinions are the product of an affirmative effort to create obfuscation and flexibility.

Long opinions may be unnecessarily so; higher quality work could have been done in shorter space and time. For example, when I requested a brief pamphlet to explain our voluminous cable television rules to the small cable operators and public, the commissioners and staff refused to prepare it. (The staff lawyers who had created the lengthy document soon left the Commission and began charging cable operators legal fees for explanations.)

Another issue is the regularity with which major FCC decisions are reported in the trade press days before they are announced to the public. This can affect stock prices, constitute violations of law and good administrative practice. It stands in stark contrast to the Supreme Court's control of leaks and throws into question the propriety of the FCC's process.

From the Supreme Court I went to the faculty of the University of California at Berkeley ("Boalt Hall") for three years. I wrote the major law review article expected of all new professors ("Producer Rate Regulation in Natural Gas Certification Proceedings: Catco in Context," *Columbia Law Review* (1962)), created a casebook of teaching materials (unpublished), and was put through teaching the usual *potpourri* of courses: administrative law, administrative law seminar, business associations, corporations, equity, and oil and gas law.

Boalt Hall was and is by any standard one of our country's best law schools in terms of faculty and student body. It was yet another opportunity to be associated with first-class minds and serious research – in the law school and throughout the University. Dean Bill Prosser (torts) headed the school when I was hired, but I won't go through the names of all the faculty – many of whom are well-known nationally and internationally within the academy. My principal interest soon focused on administrative law, and that meant a chance to work with the energized Renaissance man and newly-chosen Dean Frank Newman.

For most people, most of the time, "law" means what some civil servant is requiring them to do: pay taxes, pass driver's license tests, qualify for a beauty shop license, zoning permit, license to sell alcohol, or pay the regulated telephone rates. The success of our legal system is dependent upon the fair and efficient functioning of our administrative agencies.

This revelation provided a logical melding of my interests in political science and law and proved to be an insight into things to come. I spent one summer studying the California Public Service Commission and came to know and work with others in the administrative law field such as Ken Davis, Walter Gellhorn, and Louis Jaffe. But I soon came to realize my academic studies of administrative law were not adequate for what I wanted to research, write and teach. I needed to add the hands-on experience of practicing administrative law.

Covington & Burling, where I had spent the summer of 1957 as a law student, had flattered me with repeated offers – after graduation, the clerkship with Judge Brown, the clerkship with Justice Black, and while at Boalt Hall. Their interest was such that they were willing to take me on leave from Berkeley for two years to work on administrative agency matters. It was the largest firm in Washington and had an extensive administrative practice. It prided itself on the number of former Supreme Court law clerks working there, and partners who would go in and out of government. So much so that it was sometimes jokingly referred to as "one of the larger government agencies."

Much has been written about Covington & Burling by those who study the large corporate law firms in Washington and New York, At the time I worked there (1963-64) it was still housed in the Union Trust Building at 15th and H Streets in downtown Washington. (The firm later succumbed to the lure of modern office buildings and moved down the street to the new Motion Picture Association of America Building – a couple blocks from the White House, near the AFL-CIO building, Lafayette Park and Hay Adams Hotel.) The halls were dark, furniture and rugs were old, offices were small and hard to find, and dictating equipment had not yet arrived. The 100 or so lawyers wore vests and short-cropped hair and preferred 30-second bursts of phone conversation to five-minute office visits. They made millions of dollars for themselves and probably billions for their clients.

The apocryphal story is told of how large legal fees began. In the very early days of the firm the new young lawyers (now senior partners) were trying to decide how much to bill a corporate client for some litigation and drafting of legal papers. They finally screwed up their courage and asked the secretary to prepare a bill for $5,000. Anxiously awaiting whether it would be protested or paid, they were surprised when the return mail produced a check, not for $5,000 but for $50,000. Upon inquiry, they found the secretary had inadvertently added an additional zero and they were $45,000 richer. They have been adding an additional zero ever since and have seldom if ever received a complaint.

They are, quite simply, the best lawyers in the business — "lawyers' lawyers" they're called. They seldom become involved in a case until some other firm has made a mess of things, comes to them for advice, or a corporate client is in over its head.

Such clients are occasionally engaged in somewhat less than savory practices. They want to go on manufacturing the drugs that the Food and Drug Administration says are hazardous to health; advertise in ways the Federal Trade Commission says are false and misleading; dump waste products into rivers the Environmental Protection Agency says they're polluting; drill offshore after they've spilled oil on beaches; build the Alaskan Pipeline; strip mine for coal and clear cut for timber; raise permitted airline rates from the Civil Aeronautics Board; and lower taxes from the Internal Revenue Service. It takes

lawyers to obtain permission for their
ﾝgage in these highly profitable practices.
ﾗﾄ ﾗﾙe 1950s and early 1960s representing
corporate clients in such ventures did not create the
moral conflict for lawyers that it tends to today. What
we today call the consumer or environmental
movements didn't exist. Now there are at least small
activist organizations, academic literature and small
circulation magazines. Then a lawyer might never be
confronted with a question of conscience, his (it was
almost never a her) impact upon the Earth and the
life it sustains. There was professional pride in the
quality of one's work, regardless of substance or
impact; a satisfaction in the skillful use of one's
talents. If the issue of propriety was ever raised, there
could always be the lawyer's response: every client
deserves the best representation available. There
was reverence for process, and pride in one's
ideological neutrality. In fairness, during the era of
Senator Joseph McCarthy's communist witch hunts
many of these same lawyers were defending, often
pro bono (without pay), those whose careers were
being destroyed by mere allegations. If pressed they
would probably feel a total consistency in their
actions. They hung out a shingle to represent
whoever came along. Just as some doctors
specialize in diseases of the rich while volunteering
in free clinics, these lawyers specialize in the legal
diseases of America's wealthiest corporations while
occasionally serving the deserving poor *pro bono*.

In fairness, Covington & Burling and many
other law firms are not involved with their clients'

political action – though they may prepare legal analyses for documents used by lobbyists. These lawyers do not lobby or carry cash to senators, hold off-the-record meetings with regulatory commissioners about pending cases, or schedule industry price-fixing meetings. The "lawyer-lobbyist" is a special breed in Washington.

Whatever the original intent of those who wrote the Constitution, the net effect has been that the very best legal talent is arrayed on the side of corporations and their wealthy owners. Little is devoted to representing the interests of consumers, taxpayers, television viewers, or other concerns of ordinary citizens. In fairness to the large firms, many have provided the lawyers who were sent out or opted out to establish the public interest law firms. They were among the first to offer lawyers to legal aid clinics. They have fought for small claims courts, court-appointed representation of criminals and other indigents. Many have not opposed the creation of Neighborhood Legal Services or the Consumer Protection Agency even though their clients might.

The fact is that most of the efforts of consumer, environmental and other public interest organizations are directed at undoing what large law firms have done on behalf of their clients. And because the law graduates recruited by the large firms are, by definition, among the brightest and best educated young men and women our nation can produce, many of whom like to think of themselves as liberal to radical, they must confront the inherent conflict between their ideals and their jobs.

Some resolve the problem by adopting the entire corporate lifestyle (expensive clothes, country clubs, vacation homes, travel). Some salve their conscience by returning each evening to their former lives of long hair, bell-bottom jeans and pot. A few insist on spending significant portions of their time (and firm's resources) on *pro-bono* cases, fighting the very class of clients (though not the same clients) the rest of the firm is defending. Those unable to resolve the conflict leave for public interest law firms, government jobs or teaching.

When I joined the firm for a two-year term I had no more sophistication and social conscience than other attorneys. The firm was representing tobacco companies the lawyers called "the cancer lobby," though I did not do so. The companies sought to avoid governmental inhibitions on the sale of cigarettes: the Surgeon General's warning ("cigarette smoking is hazardous to your health"), the ban on advertising, or a possible ban on sales. I did not smoke and was even less inclined to start once learning all the young attorneys working on the cancer lobby account had quit smoking by the time I left the firm. I did not want to work on that project and would not have done so. But my lack of sophistication about the role of American corporate power was such that many accounts struck me as ethically and morally neutral. Today their negative influence would be more obvious.

What I primarily ended up working on (in addition to representing the small airline Panagra, and the Venezuelan government regarding a ship seized in Philadelphia) was antidumping legislation. Businessmen tend to praise the theory of competition but use pejoratives to describe its practice when it threatens to move in next door. For example, the Bell Telephone Company referred to any competitor's telephone equipment as "foreign attachments." Similarly, our clients, American manufacturers of steel and cement, referred to the ultracompetitive pricing of steel or cement from abroad as "dumping."

There is some rationale for antidumping laws. "Dumping" is defined as selling goods in a foreign market below the price in the manufacturer's domestic market, sometimes even below the cost of manufacturing. Usually this is done to obtain a larger market share, or even drive some competitors out of the market. But it is a complicated matter indeed to settle upon a fair price when there is a dispute. And antidumping laws can be abused as a means of driving out all foreign competition.

Our clients retained Covington & Burling to represent their interests with regard to the importation of steel and cement from Japan and elsewhere at prices believed by them to violate the antidumping laws.

Donald Hiss was the partner handling the account, and it was a pleasure to work with him. He was an extremely able lawyer with a sense of humor well above the average for the firm.

As the brother of Alger Hiss, he had a commitment to civil liberties and liberal causes, and my wife, Karen, had worked with Don's sister, Anna, at the University of Texas.

What attracted me to the case was the possibility of creating an administrative procedure act for antidumping cases. Administrative law was my field, and the prospect of studying the process the Treasury Department and Tariff Commission used in an esoteric area of the law like antidumping was my idea of getting paid for a good time. The bureaucratic maneuverings and relative insensitivity to rather elemental principles of due process were fascinating. Drafting a new administrative procedure act to be introduced in Congress and possibly become law was heady stuff for a 28-year-old administrative law professor.

The possibility my effort to import due process into the procedure might create an increase in the price of steel and cement in this country, lessen two basic industries' need for rapid technological innovation, and misdirect economic resources from relatively more competitive industries were matters of little concern at the time. My experience in studying the California Public Utilities Commission would have real world impact in the cause of fair procedure. It seemed to me a worthy and educational undertaking.

On November 22, 1963, I heard at lunch the news that President John F. Kennedy had been shot. ABC News maintains a window on Connecticut Avenue, and I watched the television report for a while. I asked the partner with whom I'd had lunch and been working that morning (not Don Hiss) whether we would take the afternoon off. He thought there was entirely too much sentimentality about the assassination and that it ought to be treated like any other work day. We walked back to our 15th Street office.

There is an emotional hardening that can evolve in those growing up in any profession anywhere. But it seems worse in Washington. Ultimately it got to me, until the reaction burst forth in a book I titled *Test Pattern for Living* (1972). Whether from necessity or habit, there is a commitment to long hours, rock-hard efficiency, and putting a priority on work and career above family and social contacts. It seems more prevalent in Washington law firms and government agencies than elsewhere.

I was very moved by the assassination of President Kennedy and the events live and televised surrounding it. It intensified my commitment to government service, the American dream, and my desire to participate in some way.

A couple months later I received an indirect indication that a government job might be in the offing.

Chapter Three
At Sea in Washington:
The Maritime Administration

It has never been clear to me exactly how my name came to President Johnson's attention – who first suggested it to whom, and why, and what was then done about it. Because my name was Johnson, and I had graduated from the University of Texas, many people assumed I was either a relative or an old-time friend of the President's. Neither was true. Presidential appointees are designated by their home states; my designation was Iowa.

I never met the President until our 1964 meeting in the Oval Office. Nor had I known any senator or member of congress, party campaign contributor, or any of his former or present friends or colleagues.

The story went around, and appeared in some newspapers, that Bill Moyers and I had been roommates in Austin, and that it was he who urged my appointment on the President. The fact is that Bill and I were both married and living with our wives while at the University of Texas and that we never met until after my appointment.

In fact, later reports were that Bill Moyers was the only one on the White House staff who expressed hesitation about the appointment. Bill, a principal advisor to the President at 29, felt the Maritime Administrator's job might be too much for a 29-year-old. Without any comment from him, there is no more reason to believe it true than newspaper stories asserting the contrary.

Bill Moyers did play an unintended role in my appointment. Another story will put it in context.

A fellow called the White House and asked to speak to Jack Valenti, another presidential advisor and assistant. Once the conversation began the caller realized he was talking to the President and apologized, "I'm terribly sorry, Mr. President, I didn't mean to bother you, I was calling Jack Valenti." "Oh, that's all right," drawled back the President, "Jack's busy this afternoon and I'm taking his calls."

There was a phone message on my desk at Covington & Burling one day informing me of a forthcoming meeting with Bill Moyers. Never having been in the West Wing before, I arrived a little early, was ushered through the gate by the guards, and told to wait in a West Wing reception area outside the press offices. It was exciting just to be there watching aides to the President and journalists, some of whom were recognizable from television, going about their tasks.

As time wore on it became somewhat less exciting – fifteen minutes, a half hour, finally an hour slipped by. It was an introduction to the pressures of officials' schedules, their relative insensitivity to callers, that mark much of official Washington – and into which I would soon find myself sliding.

Suddenly, through the door bounded the bundle of smiles and energy known as Jack Valenti. He quickly introduced himself, asked that I follow him, and we went dashing through corridors of the White House. He opened a door, motioned to me to enter, turned and left.

When I looked up I realized I was in the Oval Office of the President, alone with President Johnson. As if a forecast of things to come, he was watching a television screen in the three-TV console given him by Frank Stanton of CBS – perhaps something taped for him earlier. Apparently President Johnson was not only willing to take Jack Valenti's calls but Bill Moyers' visitors as well.

The surrealism of the experience left very little memory of our conversation. We probably talked for fifteen or twenty minutes. He said he wanted to nominate me as Maritime Administrator, and told me something of the industry, the agency, his plans for it, and how I should go about getting through my Senate hearings. He had an impressive depth of understanding of maritime matters. Throughout subsequent months his grasp of current details whenever we talked – even at social events when he could not have been briefed in advance – continued to amaze me.

The Maritime Administration is not one of the more prominent agencies in Washington. Despite an early interest in government, a political science major, law school course in administrative law, specializing in teaching and practice of administrative law, I had never heard of the Maritime Administration. Even the White House staff confused it with the Maritime Commission, an entirely separate agency focused on freight rates, when addressing parcels to me.

That an agency of the federal government can take roughly $500 million a year from taxpayers and redistribute it to wealthy shipowners and shipyards for thirty years without ever coming to public consciousness is commentary on the ills of Washington and its press corps – discussed at greater length below.

The Maritime Administration offered considerable challenge. During the first weeks in office there was ongoing discovery of additional responsibilities and titles. The Administrator is also chair of a Maritime Subsidy Board, adjudicating disputes between the agency and its beneficiaries. As Commandant of the Maritime Service the Administrator is given three-star admiral rank, a personal flag, and responsibility for a four-year academy at Kings Point, New York – the maritime version of Annapolis and West Point – for training merchant marine officers. It's not clear whether the position of Maritime Administrator still carried the title of Director, War Shipping Authority. In any event, during Vietnam War buildup we worked with the Pentagon's Military Sea Transportation Service (MSTS) and Secretary of the Navy, drawing the Maritime Administration's World War II merchant ships out of mothballs to operate what was the world's largest shipping company. (The Maritime Administration has responsibility for overseeing and removing rust from about 2,000 Liberty and Victory ships in Reserve Fleets around America's seacoasts.) The Administrator also chairs the NATO merchant shipping conference, Planning Board for Ocean Shipping (PBOS). The agency played a role in shipping surplus grain abroad under the PL-480 program and designed and built fishing boats and other craft for government agencies.

The principal tasks were dispensing hundreds of millions of dollars of subsidy and low-cost loans to

American merchant shipping companies and shipyards.

While leaving the White House, following the meeting with the President, I was probably flattered, thrilled and certain to accept – though I cannot recall what I was thinking subconsciously. Later there were doubts about accepting. It was not clear why the President wanted to appoint me to this position. Was it possible some scandal was about to break for which I'd be the fall guy?

It later became more obvious that President Johnson was prescient enough to know, confronted with a short list of 15 or 20 individuals who *wanted* to be Maritime Administrator, and knowing of the ties between the industry and the agency, that the most important qualification was an individual who did *not* want the job. That may have been my only qualification.

My plan had been to come to Washington to study and practice administrative law and return to teaching. Government service was quite a departure from that career plan. Moreover, aside from not wanting the job would I have the other qualifications, skills and experience required?

Some questioned the President's choice. Following the President's announcement of the appointment Pierre Salinger, the President's Press Secretary, was asked at his morning press briefing if it was true the young Administrator-nominee was born in 1934. Salinger replied, "There's nothing wrong with 1934. It was a good year, a vintage year." There was no more questioning of my youth.

Objections to appointees usually focus on their lack of knowledge and experience rather than their age. As an Iowa boy my shipping knowledge was zero. As I freely conceded to the Senate Commerce Committee members the President had asked me to call upon, it consisted of a couple unnoteworthy canoe trips on the Iowa River of less than one mile. This bothered neither them nor me at the time – nor since, when I evaluate the appointment to other positions of those with scant experience.

There are many professions in which one is repeatedly forced to deal with wholly new bodies of knowledge. The law is but one. For example, representation of steel, cement and airline companies at Covington & Burling required cram courses in those industries, as the FCC appointment required quick study of broadcasting, telephone operations, communications satellites, under-ocean cables, and other industries new to me.

Other professions require this ability. Journalists must quickly acquire enough background to understand the story they're reporting. Architects must understand by whom, how, and why their buildings will be used. Economists know more than the financial structure of industries they're studying.

What I needed to know about shipping – enough to ask, and address, questions about the basics – could be learned in a couple weeks of long hours. What seemed more relevant, and went unaddressed by critics, was my total absence of business, management and administrative education and experience.

Management of large public and private institutions requires knowledge and experience often not possessed by those otherwise outstanding in their substantive field; for example, when the best research scientist in the lab is promoted to be the director.

The story is told of a newly-appointed Secretary of State's first day on the job. Two staff assistants found him writing on a yellow pad. Upon inquiry he explained that he was answering the mail. He had been a brilliant practicing lawyer in a small firm used to handling such tasks himself. The assistants patiently explained to him that all cables coming to the State Department are addressed to the Secretary of State, that there are thousands of them every day, and hundreds of people to answer them.

There is almost nothing in the experience of the ablest of professionals to prepare them for the difference between solo effort, or even managing a secretary, clerk, and half-dozen assistants, and the job of administering an institution with thousands of employees and budgets of millions or billions of dollars.

Moreover, there is no training program for Presidential appointees. The government spends millions of dollars training foreign service officers, military, and civil servants doing virtually every kind of task. But there's a presumption newly-appointed agency heads arrive knowing what to do with no need for training. Maybe career civil servants are aware it is they who are doing it all, it makes little difference who heads the agency, they've outlasted the new guy's predecessors and will outlast this one, and that they will soon enough be asked for their advice.

At that time the Maritime Administration was an agency within the Department of Commerce. A successful businessman and former governor of North Carolina, Luther Hodges, was appointed Secretary of Commerce by President John F. Kennedy in 1961. When I asked, and he told me there was no training program for presidential appointees, I followed up by asking if he had any advice for me. "Yes," he said, "just remember to pee every chance you get."

Feeling not quite fully informed I wrote some acquaintances at the Harvard Business School: "Help, please. I've never administered anything other than a single secretary, and that not very successfully. What should I do?" Back by return mail came a box containing six books and a handwritten note: "Read these books and do what they say." I did. Most observers thought it worked.

President Johnson's Administration advanced some progressive management innovation, such as the systems analysis, cost-effectiveness, and planning, programming, budgeting system (PPBS) of the then Bureau of the Budget. With credit to my new-found tutors, the Maritime Administration was among the first agencies on the civilian side of the Potomac River to adopt the new programs.

But this experience became just one more of my difficulties at the FCC. The principles of good management and administration are sensible, obvious and essential once practiced; for example, some notion of agency purpose, goals, and means to measure achievement. Such approaches are so totally alien to most government administrators, perhaps especially cabinet officers concerned with congressional testimony and speeches, that perpetual frustration awaits anyone who tries to apply them.

After developing a minimal capacity to deal with the perquisites of office, numerous titles and responsibilities, tasks of administering 2,500 employees, as many ships, and $500 million a year, my thoughts migrated to exploration of the reason for it all.

Conversations with President Johnson left little doubt that he felt the transportation industries generally, and especially the shipping industry could deliver more for the taxpayer's and shipper's dollar. Every economist told me only more confirming details for his judgment.

The maritime industry, once besieged with demands for extinction or reform, contracted an independent economic study. The 1961 book-length report by economists Allen R. Ferguson and others from the Transportation Center at Northwestern University was titled, *The Economic Value of the United States Merchant Marine.* Maritime industry leaders were confident of their worth and that the study would protect them from attacks on their subsidy programs. The report considered all aspects of shipping's economic impact, such as employment, movement of goods and balance of payments. The economists' conclusion? The last sentence of the last paragraph of the last chapter said, in effect, and thus we find there is no economic value of the United States merchant marine.

OK, the owners said, but how about the defense value of our ships? Defense Secretary Robert

McNamara and his staff repeatedly reported that there was nothing gained from these megabuck subsidies that could not be acquired better and cheaper in other ways. If Congress wants to continue them, fine, but the subsidy program is not worth one dollar of defense appropriations.

The details would require another book. But some brief definitions and examples may help.

An American flag ship is one owned by an American company, built in an American shipyard, carries an American crew, and flies an American flag. Each of these requirements costs more than its foreign equivalent, including the flag.

Building a ship in an American shipyard costs roughly twice what it would cost if purchased from a Japanese or European shipyard. The numbers and wages of American merchant seamen double the labor cost of operating an American rather than a foreign flag ship. These differences between American and foreign costs were the basis for Maritime Administration subsidies. American taxpayers were paying the difference between foreign and U.S. costs; a differential subsidy to the shipyards for ships and the shipping companies for union wages. The rationale? It was argued the subsidies bought the country ship building capacity and more control over our imports and exports.

What were Secretary McNamara's arguments? The facts were that shipyard capacity would be retained anyway because the yards were near capacity fulfilling Navy contracts. Second, when rapid, vast increases in ship building capacity were required during World War

II we were able to build thousands of low-cost merchant ships in short order. Third, those ships were still available in reserve fleets twenty years later. Fourth, the speed and size of jet planes led Secretary McNamara's analysts to conclude planes were often more cost-effective than ships for moving troops and some cargo during the Vietnam war. Finally, if we ever needed cargo ships we didn't have and couldn't produce there would be foreign shipyards to build them or ship operators willing to lease them.

How about our peacetime economy's need for trained crews and available ships? First, most American imports and exports are traveling on foreign flag ships – about 96 percent. Second, American companies have a ready worldwide market of available shipping services. Third, Americans rent automobiles, fly on airlines' planes, ship on others' railroads and trucks, and see no more need to own ships than the equipment used by other modes of transportation. Even the Defense Department uses foreign flag (American owned but foreign built and manned) ships to haul petroleum products to Vietnam. Fourth, companies that do want their own ships, such as oil company tankers, find foreign flag ships fully adequate.

Many American corporations owned foreign subsidiaries and purchased foreign made goods of all descriptions. The U.S. government sometimes encouraged "buy American" policies if prices were nearly competitive or imposed additional costs, such as tariffs or duties, on foreign goods. But the American flag rule in shipping was an absolute and total ban on importation of foreign built ships under any circumstances, whatever the price.

We manufactured airplanes in the U.S. and sold them to other countries because ours were cheaper and had improved technology. A free trade philosophy would urge that we export what we can produce best and cheapest, such as agricultural products, computer technology, machine tools, and airframes, and import what can best be produced elsewhere, such as pocket transistor radios and ships. Our American flag rules were one of the most glaring exceptions to this policy.

The Maritime Administration programs amounted to little more than taking $500 million in taxes from poor and middle-class Americans and giving it to rich shipping and shipyard corporations. The recipients gave nothing in return, or at least nothing more than Americans would have had without their contribution.

It would have been possible to cut government spending and the burden on taxpayers by a few fractions of a percent by cutting back on Maritime Administration staff or eliminating a ship or two from the budget. But the more basic question was, why are we doing this at all? Chapter One reveals this was a question I first put to the YMCA as a teenager. Now in later life it was a question usefully asked about government programs.

Shortly after my appointment as Maritime Administrator Justice Black's former law clerks gathered to celebrate his 80th birthday. We all shared a tremendous sense of affection and loyalty towards the Judge and his wife, Elizabeth. We looked forward to family occasions to gather and pay our respects.

Justice Black was appointed by President Franklin D. Roosevelt and maintained a friendship with a couple members of President Roosevelt's brain trust, Ben Cohen and Tom "Tommy the Cork" Corcoran, who also attended these affairs.

The Maritime Administration was created in 1936. The first Maritime Administrator was President Kennedy's father, Joe Kennedy. I thought Mr. Corcoran might have some advice to offer.

He did. He said I should do what Joe Kennedy had done. What was that? Kennedy served for one year during which he prepared a report. He detailed the subsidy programs and their irrationality. He proposed their elimination or at least more rational application, such as rewarding efficiency rather than inefficiency. As Corcoran characterized Joe Kennedy's report, "The maritime industry is an awful mess. If you will do what I recommend it will get better. Now please give me a different job."

President Roosevelt had been one of President Johnson's mentors. Roosevelt selected him at a tender age to head the Youth Administration in Texas. Would President Johnson be open to such an approach? As it turned out he was. But it took two reports and 28 months before my leaving, the second longest Maritime Administrator's term in history.

The Maritime Administration provided a pleasant tie to my continuing relationship with Judge John R. Brown, the former admiralty lawyer for whom I clerked, and we enjoyed the coincidence. But it also introduced me to what's wrong with Washington in general and the FCC in particular: the subgovernment phenomenon.

66 – Catfish Solution

Chapter Four
Where Have All the Taxes Gone? Subgovernments in Washington

One of the more incongruous and disappointing features of maritime policy reform is that shipping executives who shout "get the government off my back," profess support for free enterprise, Milton Friedman's economics and Barry Goldwater's politics, are among the most ferocious advocates for the maritime subsidy programs.

Shipping policy has little to do with political philosophy or intellectual analysis. It is a simple cash transfer. It was not surprising, following the Johnson Administration's efforts to cut maritime subsidies, that one of President Richard Nixon's first acts was a maritime subsidy increase of three billion dollars!

It is difficult to understand why such a program was begun, would continue, and even increase. Consider:

(1) There is an enormous amount of tax money involved.

(2) There is no benefit from the program. Economists, prone to disagreements, are united on this issue.

(3) It is hard to understand politically. For example, agricultural subsidies impact millions of farmers. Their elimination would create a political hornet's nest for senators and House members representing rural districts. By contrast, shipping

subsidies only go to a handful of districts and companies.

(4) Budget examiners at the Maritime Administration, Department of Commerce, Bureau of the Budget, White House, House and Senate Appropriations Committees go over every detail of the Maritime budget. How could a $500 million useless program slip by all of them unnoticed?

(5) What's more distressing is Maritime's program comes closer to illustrating the rule than a bizarre exception to it. Many government programs transfer money from taxpayers and consumers to a handful of individuals or corporations.

How is this done? It takes many forms.

Tariffs. An unjustified tariff may increase one company's profits. How? By forcing price increases paid by consumers on goods from a foreign competitor, which in turn enable the domestic manufacturer to increase its prices.

Cash subsidy. It may be a simple cash transfer from taxpayers to beneficiaries, such as agricultural or maritime subsidies.

Technology transfer. Airlines pay reduced prices for airplanes because of free technology transfer to civilian aircraft manufacturers from military aircraft innovations paid by taxpayers. Early airlines were subsidized by taxpayers, presumably for carrying small bags of mail. In 1974 Pan Am thought it appropriate to ask taxpayers for an additional $10 million a month to help it over hard times.

Contracts. Some government functions are contracted out. Defense Department contracts can involve billions of dollars. In 1974 it was disclosed the Northrup Corporation had a $1.2 million secret political fund. It sounds like a lot of money until you realize Northrup was competing for a $13.5 *billion* defense contract. Campaign contributions were merely an insurance premium and a very cheap one at that: less than 1/100th of one percent of a single contract.

Defense weapons systems are a questionable investment from many points of view. The hardware is virtually handcrafted and scandalously overpriced. Overruns add 10 to 50 percent to the original price. The finished product may not work. Given the rapid development of new technology it may be obsolete when delivered. If it serves its purpose it will never be used. It's a deterrent. It will only consume, never generate the revenue created by, say, a tractor or forklift truck.

Even the design phase of weapons systems are leaf raking programs for scientists and engineers. If they were paid to focus their brilliance on rapid transit, electric cars, or even vacuum cleaners they could contribute billions of dollars to the gross national product and an improved balance of trade.

It's as if we pay billions of dollars to manufacture pianos we then dump in the ocean – which in the case of the $1.3-billion Trident submarines is literally what we do.

There is less hypocrisy in maritime and airline subsidies. They do not pretend to be anything more than a transfer of money from the poor to the rich for which nothing is asked in return. Analysis of defense contracts for weapons manufacturers is more complicated because something appears to be given in return.

Rate regulation. There are also ways government enriches corporations with increases in consumer prices. For example, the FCC recently voted a telephone rate increase for AT&T. Consumers will fork over an additional $1.2 billion a year to the company for the same service they have now. The increase is unwarranted according to the FCC's Common Carrier Bureau, trial staff, hearing examiner, public groups, and my staff. A majority of commissioners voted for it anyway.

The money will be paid by poor and middle-class taxpayers as much as if the FCC had voted AT&T a $1.2 billion subsidy. But it will not be paid by them as taxpayers. They will pay it every month in higher telephone bills rather than every year in higher taxes April 15th.

The Civil Aeronautics Board pegs airline rates at twice what a free-market price might be. Tickets on an intrastate California airline the CAB cannot regulate are about four cents a mile. East coast airlines charging CAB-set rates receive 11 cents a mile. In 1974 the Federal Power Commission increased natural gas rates by 75 percent, a multi-billion-dollar increase for consumers. Its decision was overturned. Courts found the FPC had acted illegally. The Department of Agriculture sets milk prices. Following a campaign contribution, the next year consumers paid an additional $400 million for their milk.

Monopoly and oligopoly pricing. A monopoly exists if a single corporation controls a market. An oligopoly describes a market dominated by three or four firms. Sometimes money is extracted from consumers by monopolies' or oligopolies' illegal prices set, not by government, but by the corporations. Government is implicated not because of what it did but what it failed to do. It permits the excessive prices to continue without antitrust enforcement, price controls, excess profits taxes, or other regulation. The total bill to consumers is variously estimated at some $75 to $100 *billion* in excess product costs. A 1974 example: automobile demand was down by about 25 percent but prices continued their pre-planned, profit-maximizing rise.

There are other ways in which government takes money from the poor and gives it to the rich, and dozens of examples of each strategy. But this discussion of subsidies, contracts, price setting, tariffs, and unregulated oligopoly pricing is enough to provide an introductory understanding.

Subgovernments are created to bring about these results. So what are the conditions and elements creating a successful subgovernment?

The first has just been described: a government agency with the authority and opportunity to enrich a corporation or industry with millions or billions of dollars.

The second is the agency's enormous discretion as to whom it will enrich and how. The enabling legislation may say the agency is to act "in the public interest."

Third, the agency's beneficiaries must be few enough that business can be transacted on a personal basis among friends.

For example, the Federal Trade Commission and Antitrust Division of the Department of Justice do *not* perfectly fit the subgovernment mold. This is not because they are staffed with paragons of virtue seeking to find and serve an elusive public interest. It's because they don't meet the necessary conditions to grow a subgovernment.

Both the Antitrust Division and FTC can affect millions of dollars of corporate assets and profits. Both have some discretion. For example, the Antitrust Division cannot possibly move against every antitrust violation and is not legally required to evaluate and approve or disapprove every merger. Which transactions it prosecutes or ignores can make multi-million-dollar differences to corporations.

What prevents their becoming a subgovernment is the breadth of their responsibility: the entire U.S. economy. This is not to say the nation's largest corporations do not have political influence or that their officers and lobbyists are unknown to those heading both agencies. It's just that neither agency can conduct business on a personal basis among friends. This also applies to most courts, which also have tradition and other reasons to avoid morphing into subgovernments. Their jurisdiction is so broad they are not dealing with the kind of small, specialized clientele that frequent industry-specific regulatory commissions.

Many regulatory commissions and executive branch agencies do develop a subgovernment. They tend to deal with a single industry, such as railroads, gas pipelines, coal, airlines, telephones, broadcasting, oil, or shipyards.

What are the other characteristics of subgovernments? They tend to be relatively constant. So rather than burdening the reader with fulsome descriptions of every industry's subgovernment, and because this book focuses on the FCC, the broadcasting subgovernment will be used as an example.

First, oligopoly. Subgovernments often involve monopolies and oligopolies. An oligopoly is a small group of large companies (often three) with disproportionate control over an entire industry. In broadcasting the oligopoly's members are the three networks: ABC, CBS and NBC. Networks have hundreds of affiliates broadcasting network programs. In addition, they each own TV stations in the largest markets. Those 15 stations (out of 700 nationally) earn about half the industry's total gross revenue and have an equally disproportionate share of its political power. There are a handful of multiple-station owners, such as Westinghouse, RKO General and Metromedia, but none compares with the networks.

Second, spokesperson. Whatever the industry there is often one respectable spokesperson. He, it's always a he, is usually college educated, possessed of a respectable image, and trotted out when a major pronouncement or congressional testimony is required. For broadcasting Dr. Frank Stanton was the man. Since his departure the position has been vacant notwithstanding Arthur Taylor's efforts to fill it.

Third, trade associations. Trade associations are the front organizations for the dominant firms. Broadcasting's trade association is unimaginatively designated as the National Association of Broadcasters (NAB). The primary purpose of trade associations, in this case NAB, is to do things for the dominant firms that will help them but would harm the networks' reputations if done in their name. The NAB also substantially expands their political base.

There are limits to the political influence of individual corporations, even those in this wealthy oligopoly controlling the nation's most powerful mass media. There are occasions when the networks need to exert influence over an individual member of Congress, governor or mayor. On those occasions they need a national constituency.

The NAB provides it. Unaware of the extent to which they are being used, small radio and television station owners join the NAB, receive publications that rewrite FCC releases, attend a massive annual convention, get free drinks, mingle with TV stars, and consider themselves more professional. In exchange the networks can benefit from political activism when they need it not only from the 15 stations they own but some 8,000 small radio and television stations owners.

The top employees of NAB have few complaints. They are provided handsome salaries and expense accounts. The dues NAB charges are enough there is a sufficient surplus to build a high-rise, multi-million-dollar mausoleum complete with fountain on Connecticut Avenue in downtown Washington, D.C. The only condition of employment is that when instances arise, as they do, when the interests of small broadcasters conflict with those of the dominant firms, the small broadcasters will be sold out in negotiations at the White House, Congress or FCC.

Fourth, trade press. The fourth major element of a subgovernment is its trade magazines. For broadcasting the dominant publication is called *Broadcasting magazine*. Another trade publication, the *Television Digest* weekly newsletter, often has even better sources.

Every organization has a journal of some kind – political parties, churches, credit unions, and scholarly societies – and subgovernments are no exception. Their journals are called the trade press and sometimes contain revealing information. They may report the industry's collection and investment of political contributions, strategies to evade regulations of unsafe drugs, exorbitant profits and consumer deception. Trade magazines contain a lot of advertising. At one time the *Oil and Gas Journal* had the most advertising of any publication measured by some standards. *Broadcasting* does well financially.

One reason for the advertising is the access it provides advertisers to publishers, editors and reporters willing to share inside information. *Broadcasting* personnel get information even FCC commissioners don't have. It goes to press Friday night for Monday a.m. delivery. (Some subscribers are favored with late night Friday or early morning Saturday copies.) Commission meetings are on Wednesdays. It's not unusual for the Monday issue to report items that will be on the commissioners' Wednesday agenda – though staff does not make them available to the commissioners until Tuesday. On one occasion when the FCC was especially troubled by leaks it turned out that the secretary to the Chief of the Broadcast Bureau was married to the chief editorial writer for *Broadcasting* magazine. FCC chairmen investigate leaks and occasionally threaten prosecution but almost always back down.

Insider information can have great economic value. If a sale is about to be approved by the Commission, a license renewed, or a station fined it can affect thousands or even millions of dollars. Stock prices may be affected. If a $10,000 purchase of advertising can enable an owner to get information three or four days before the rest of the industry it can be worth many times that $10,000. It's just good insurance.

Fifth, lawyers. A fifth component of a subgovernment is the lawyers whose practice is primarily limited to one industry and regulatory agency. They often organize their own bar association. For broadcasting they call it the Federal Communications Bar Association (FCBA); the Federal Power Commission practitioners call themselves the Federal Power Bar Association.

There is very little law involved in their practice, in terms of what students study in law school, or analytical creativity in crafting an appellate court brief. Many formerly worked for the FCC. Much of their job consists of filling out the forms they processed when an FCC employee and then visiting with their friends and former colleagues at the Commission to see how the processing is coming along.

There may be rare occasions when FCC decisions are appealed to the U.S. Court of Appeals for the District of Columbia Circuit, or even more rarely to the U.S. Supreme Court, but even they involve a relatively limited body of law.

Practice before the FCC may not involve rigorous legal analysis, but it does require mastery of some very intricate practices and customs. Much of the information is not publicly available. For years the list of FM frequencies available for new stations was kept in an FCC employee's bottom desk drawer. Clients' fortunes may turn on the discretionary whim of an FCC employee. FCBA members thereby create and preserve for themselves the reality as well as illusion of indispensability in representing a client's interests before what is in theory and could be in fact a public agency.

Sixth, interrelationships. Members of subgovernments must eat, and preferably with each other. Subgovernments have eating clubs: a Petroleum Club, Aviation Club, and of course a Broadcasters' Club. These luncheon clubs are more significant symbolically than in fact. Washington's old, prestige clubs are the Metropolitan Club (for those with money), Cosmos Club (for those with brains), and Federal City Club (for those under 60). The club scene is increasingly *passé*, and the Broadcasters' Club is a place I would never go willingly until the last McDonalds closed. The publisher of *Broadcasting* magazine, Sol Taishoff, owns both *Broadcasting*'s building and the next-door Broadcasters' Club building. He took me to lunch on two or three occasions until we discovered we agreed on virtually nothing. He never suggested the Broadcasters' Club.

It does do some business. It's used for receptions for newly appointed FCC commissioners. With seven commissioners serving seven-year terms that's at least one reception a year. But this should not diminish its symbolic significance.

Some of the most important qualities of subgovernments are their group pressures, sociological makeup, and members' interpersonal relationships. Most subgovernment gatherings are free to the attendees; half paid for by corporate employers and half by taxpayers as "ordinary and necessary business expenses." It makes little difference who puts on the event – NAB, NBC, *Broadcasting*, Broadcasters' Club, or Federal Communications Bar Association. Regardless of the ostensible sponsor they are all subgovernment events bringing together the same people eating the same shrimp. Subgovernment members' professional and social lives are intertwined. They can move freely from one broadcasting subgovernment institution to another; a publicist or journalist might move from the FCC, to a network, to a congressional office. They literally intermarry. This helps subgovernments become even more self-protective and insular than they otherwise might be, always at the ready when the wagons need circular placement.

Seventh, Congress' subcommittees. The relevant Senate and House subcommittees have a major role in the subgovernment.

Most school children who have gone beyond the "three equal branches of government" myth know this. But few Americans know its practical effect.

With rare exception most members of the Senate and House, to the extent they have any time to follow what a couple hundred committees and subcommittees are doing, focus on those for which they are a member. This is not to say they are irresponsible. Some are; most aren't. In addition to their daily hours of dialing for dollars they may put in inordinate hours of homework and committee attendance largely unnoticed by the media and constituents.

It's just that, other than those in the handful in leadership positions, most members do little of legislative consequence outside of their own committees. Moreover, unless the member is the committee chair, or ranking member, there will be little done even in the committee. Committees and subcommittees tend to be run by their chairs and a trusted staff assistant or two of the chair. As a result, what's thought to be congressional policy is disproportionately the product of an unelected handful of persons in the Senate and House. Obviously, these staff people are an important component of any industry's subgovernment.

The Senate looks to Senator Warren Magnuson, Chairman of the Senate Commerce Committee, for matters involving regulatory commissions. If the issue involves the FCC and broadcasting subgovernment, Senator Magnuson looks to Senator John Pastore, Chairman of the Communications Subcommittee of the Senate Commerce Committee. Senator Pastore, in turn, looks to his staff aide, Nicholas Zapple, to handle most of the Senator's relations with government, industry and public; preparations for hearings; legislation and budgets involving communications matters.

As a result, for most matters involving broadcasting Nicholas Zapple *is* the United States Senate. To clarify, this is not to say that Zapple has any greater power over communications policy than any other individual member of the broadcasting subgovernment. Indeed, central to the subgovernment analysis is the assertion that political power in Washington resides, not in the White House or Capitol, but in industry-oriented subgovernments made up of representatives of many institutions working in concert on a given industry's behalf. Zapple *is* the Senate only in the sense that, to the extent the Senate is one of those institutions he is its representative.

For the Maritime Administration the relevant House committee in the shipping subgovernment was the House Merchant Marine and Fisheries Committee. Its members were primarily drawn from districts with seagoing ports, shipyards, or other connections to the industry. The committee's purpose was to protect the shipping and ship building subsidies and the jurisdiction of the committee.

By contrast, for the broadcasting subgovernment Congressman Harley Staggers of West Virginia is Chairman of the House Interstate and Foreign Commerce Committee. Because Staggers has no television stations and few radio stations in his district he has proved himself something of an exception to the subgovernment pattern. Periodically he would take after the FCC for its most egregious excesses: a case finding fraud consistent with the public interest, another approving simultaneous transfer of five construction permits, and an instance of FCC Chairman Dean Burch wiretapping one of his own employees. Chairman Staggers' behavior is uncharacteristic of a subgovernment.

As a result, he provided evidence of the supremacy of the broadcasting subgovernment over the House and Senate. He once tried to get the House to find Dr. Frank Stanton in contempt of his Committee. The House refused; something that had never formerly been denied a committee chair.

Eighth, the bureau. The final component of a subgovernment is the bureau or office that has the discretion to dispense financial benefits to companies. It is occasionally, but seldom, an agency. With broadcasting the power is held by the Chief of the Broadcast Bureau. Few broadcast matters ever come to the attention of commissioners. Those that do are approved by the Bureau Chief, come with his or her recommendation, and a draft Commission opinion for commissioners to read, vote on and issue. Whether they read it or not, they generally do as he says.

The Broadcast Bureau Chief's power was highlighted for me at an annual dinner of the radio and television correspondents' association, paid for by network executives. The president sometimes attends and the cabinet and Senate and House leadership always attend. An elaborate directory is printed up for the occasion numbering all the tables and cross-indexing all attendees by name and table. The directory is relevant because low numbered tables are placed up front. The ostensible sponsor of a table has his or her name in boldface type. There is a bargaining among the networks, I understand, as to which one gets to invite various guests. It's like the pro football season draft choices: a table host can swap a senator for two House members, three FCC GS-12 employees for a GS-15.

Pretending to be a sociologist, it appeared the directory would provide a good indicator of broadcasting industry perception of power in the broadcasting subgovernment. That year Senator Pastore had introduced legislation pushed by the broadcasters, S. 2004. With public groups challenging FCC renewal of mediocre broadcasters' licenses, S. 2004 virtually insured everyone's license would be renewed and thereby calmed broadcasters' nerves. Surely Pastore would be their favorite hero of the evening.

A quick scan of the directory revealed he would be sitting at table four. This was perplexing. If Senator Pastore was sent off to table four who, pray tell, could possibly be at table one?

Table one, the directory revealed, was reserved for the highest bidder who chose someone named George Smith. And who was George Smith? He was neither a senator nor an FCC commissioner. George Smith was then Chief, Broadcast Bureau, Federal Communications Commission. George Smith was King of the Broadcasting Subgovernment – at least for that evening.

So that's the subgovernment; the broadcasting subgovernment or any other industry's subgovernment: the industry's oligopoly and other companies, industry spokespersons, trade association, trade press, bar association, social club, congressional subcommittees, and government bureau. There may be additional hangers on, such as lobbyists and public relations firms. There may be minor variations from industry to industry, such as the conscientious Congressman Harley Staggers. But the basic pattern holds for all.

These are the groups that have the real power in Washington, the individuals who shape our economic and other laws, regulations, and policies. It's not the White House, Congress, courts, or press, though all play a role. It's primarily the single-industry-focused subgovernments.

Ironically, with all the reporting from Washington, political science texts, non-fiction and novels touching on Washington power, the subgovernment phenomenon is seldom if ever explained in full. It is the least-reported major, continuous, floating scandal in town.

Many newspapers do little if any investigative journalism. It's understandable. Investigative journalism requires the very best journalists. It takes hours, sometimes months, to develop a potential story that may fizzle out. It's expensive. But it's what a democracy must have.

The easier path is to take the press conference and press release handouts, do a little editing, and pass them along to readers as the public official would wish.

If a government official accepts a ride in a company jet, or spends an exorbitant amount refurbishing an office, the few investigative reporters who remain have an uncanny ability for ferreting out the facts and reporting them. But not so much if a government agency is regularly handing out favors to its subgovernment members that are irrational, ill considered, and in violation of the public interest. Isn't the process by which this occurs newsworthy?

It was discovered that members of the Federal Power Commission held stock in natural gas companies. That was big news. But the fact they consistently voted to increase natural gas rates above reasonable levels attracted little attention. Of course, officials shouldn't hold stock in companies they regulate. Among other reasons, it's illegal. But it's unlikely stock ownership figured significantly if at all, in the FPC's decisions. The subgovernment did. But the stock ownership got reported and the subgovernment's existence and influence did not.

Not only do subgovernments exist without public knowledge of them, each of the members has a public identity with some institution. A member of Congress is perceived as such, not as a member of the maritime, oil, or broadcasting subgovernment. An employee of the FCC is seen as such, and perhaps as an industry advocate, but not as a fraternal member of the secret order that is that industry's subgovernment. Similarly, non-subgovernment friends and neighbors of FCBA members most likely think of them as simply Washington lawyers.

Despite their home institution, members of a subgovernment often have their strongest personal identification and loyalty to that subgovernment. When in conflict, a broadcasting trade magazine might support the interests of broadcasters over those of magazine publishers. Congressional members of the broadcasting subgovernment would be unlikely to support proposals for free radio and TV time for candidates – even though it would save them and their colleagues having to raise funds primarily used to buy air time. The FCC public information office might advocate proposals helping the broadcasting subgovernment trade press even though they inconvenience the FCC and public. The Broadcast Bureau will support less regulation of broadcasters rather than what's claimed to be the typical bureaucratic response: more regulation as a rationale for larger budgets and staff.

Many members of the broadcasting subgovernment have worked for more than one component of the subgovernment. A reporter for a trade magazine came to work for the FCC's public information office. Broadcast executives are appointed as commissioners and are hired as consultants. Many, perhaps most, members of the Federal Communications Bar Association once worked at the FCC. One of the attractions of the FCC for young lawyers is the possibility of being hired by an FCBA firm or broadcasting company. The Commission used to engage the protective practice of an agreement to hire back, at a larger salary, any employee who tried to make it on the outside and couldn't. Commissioners may be hired to head trade associations or practice law in FCBA firms.

Part of the broadcasting industry's leverage over commissioners comes from its political and economic influence over their appointment, reappointment, and opportunity for top salary jobs in industry and law firms. Ralph Nader dubbed this "the deferred bribe."

Membership in a subgovernment comes with pressure to conform. It would be impossible for an FCBA member to advocate a proposal that the FCC cut the permissible time for commercials by one-half. He or she would lose clients, no longer get inside information from *Broadcasting* employees, find it takes longer to get FCC forms processed, and be unable to find a golf or luncheon partner. An FCC employee who did it would find promotions harder to come by.

Because of this environment, over time one's thought processes change. Subgovernment members develop a group mind; they really do think alike. That is the threat from subgovernments: the continuous, subtle influence of industry-think on government-think and therefore public policy.

It's not that a company executive or lobbyist tried to bribe a public official with money, fishing trip, or use of a company plane – though that occurs and won't hurt the company's cause. "You can't buy my vote with a lunch," brag many officials. They are probably right; you can't. What they neglect to add is that nobody needs to buy their vote. They will vote that way anyway.

The tendency of government officials to vote the interests of their subgovernment is reinforced by formal proceedings and agency process. The subgovernments function inside the District of Columbia's boundaries. It is unusual for anyone who is not part of a subgovernment to participate in Washington decision making. Most Americans live elsewhere. They are unaware of what's going on within the agencies (mainstream media don't report it), they would not know how to participate (subgovernment lawyers have made it overly complicated), and they have neither the free days nor money to spend time in Washington.

Most FCC proceedings do not involve conflict, even between members of the subgovernment. A corporation asks for something – a construction permit, license renewal, or permission to sell a station – and the FCC eventually gets around to giving it what it wants. If there is more than one party the FCC can sit on the case for years until one of the parties gives up and settles.

Throughout this process FCC commissioners and employees hear almost exclusively from members of the subgovernment: phone calls, letters, personal visits, social occasions, legal briefs and pleadings, economic and other studies. Legal and other material can cost over $100,000 to prepare. Networks and the telephone company can afford to hire the very best minds willing to do their bidding. Very seldom is there input from independent academic studies, churches, unions, consumer groups, or other government agencies, such as the Antitrust Division of the Department of Justice.

Because commissioners and FCC employees do not read many books from independent sources, or attend academic conferences, their input is almost exclusively shaped by the subgovernment. The most outrageous assertions can find their way into stated or unstated premises for FCC action. For example, broadcasters successfully argued at one time that if cable television was not restrained it would cause all television stations to go dark. None felt compelled to ask, let alone answer where the cable industry would then find enough programming to fill all those channels.

The agency, inundated with thousands of pages of industry material, scarcely has the manpower to read, analyze and challenge it. The FCC undertook an inquiry into the impact of the new (by then ten-year old) computer industry on telecommunications. The filings were so exotic and voluminous it had to contract with Stanford Research Institute to read them. It then had to hire someone to read aloud from the Stanford report to the assembled commissioners. Notwithstanding the report, they usually ended up largely supporting their old friend Ma Bell (AT&T) whenever its interests conflicted with those of the computer industry.

The point is, for a subgovernment to inundate an agency with a single viewpoint is as influential and wrong as providing commissioners with wine, women and song.

My first awareness of the subgovernment phenomenon came from Maritime Administration experiences. Those impressions were reinforced at the Federal Communications Commission. They form the basis for much of what follows, including the recommendations for reform.

Chapter Five
First Impressions: "There Ain't No New Post Office Building"

Most presidential appointees end up serving two-year terms. As Maritime Administrator, my 28-month tour of duty was the second longest tenure in the agency's history. The reasons undoubtedly vary, but the average remains constant.

(1) Maybe there is only the illusion of government. The jobs are so complicated it takes one or two years to accomplish anything. Is there a grand design to move presidential appointees every two years to insure nothing will get done? Is it safer to leave it in the hands of civil servants?

(2) For some appointees the job requires such a significant cut in pay they can't afford more than two years.

(3) Some are so ambitious to climb the ladder they've never done anything for more than two years.

(4) There is another government appointment they want, and they've figured out how to get it.

(5) Others find they don't like the work; they want out of government.

(6) Some burn out; they're too exhausted to be of much use.

There is another factor at work for a reformer at the Maritime Administration, or other agencies in a subgovernment

Within limits, presidential appointees write their own job descriptions. Mine was to improve the efficiency of America's shipping companies, shipyards, ports, and shipping policy to assist our economy, balance of payments, and welfare of Americans. For a maritime subgovernment very comfortable with how things are, thank you, this was not a shared mission.

My goals took the form of the following.

Shipping subsidies should provide incentives for efficiency rather than inefficiency; ultimately ships and shipyards operating with no need for subsidies.

Upon discovering 90 percent of the cost of moving goods across the ocean is incurred within 10 miles of each port, I proposed container ships – loading semi trucks' intermodal containers onto railroad flatcars and then ships. A trucking operator, Malcolm McLean, was willing to offer such a service across the Atlantic with no subsidy.

Money for research and development could pay dividends. Operating ships above the water's surface cut drag, thereby improving both efficiency and speed. For example, hydrofoil (suspended on underwater foils) and surface effect (suspended on air) ships could offer a cargo service halfway in speed and cost between slow ships and overnight air freight.

Years later many of the proposals were accepted by the industry: larger, faster ships; more automation; ships' officers trained to work as both engineers and deck officers; container ships; barge-carrying ships; phasing out subsidy-laden passenger ships; and efficiencies in shipyards based on Japanese and Swedish experience.

At the time, however, it was too much, too fast; a threat to the maritime subgovernment. There were calls for my resignation every six months. The timing was so regular it was almost as if the industry set up tickler file reminders. President Johnson was supportive through each of these attacks. It was rumored he was offered $200,000 in campaign contributions to move me out and refused the offer. In private word and public act he saw to it the industry understood he did not intend to remove me.

Justice Black took an interest in my work as Maritime Administrator. He had investigated shipping subsidy scandals when a U.S. Senator (1927-1937). During his lifetime he offered me counsel on personal and professional matters. After the first call for my resignation he was all smiles. "I'm relieved," he said. "What do you mean?" I replied. "Well, I always thought you were an honest man, but it's still nice to have a confirmation. As long as they're still after you I'll know you're doing an honest job as Administrator."

President Franklin D. Roosevelt's man, Tommy "The Cork" Corcoran, responded with a longer story. He told me New England fishermen had difficulty keeping their catch alive on the way back to the dock. They tried flushing water through the hold where the fish were kept. They tried ice. Nothing seemed to work. In desperation they tried, and found their answer to be, putting a sea catfish in with the other fish. The catfish would go to the bottom of the hold, squirm around looking for food, and every so often jab one of the other fish with its fin spines. The stung fish would come to life, wiggle, swim through the rest, keeping them moving, and alive. "That's your job," Mr. Corcoran said. "You're that catfish. You're supposed to keep the rest of those old dying fish alive. Go ahead and poke them. It's good for them."

There were some in the Johnson Administration, the academy, the media and elsewhere who understood what I was doing and its utility. My view was that power is to be used, if used for constructive ends, regardless of the adverse impact on my career.

It was a view shared by the President. The story is told that one of Johnson's aides opposed his push for the Civil Rights Act. "You should not lay the prestige of the presidency on the line," he said. The President reportedly replied, "What's it for it it's not to be laid on the line?" That attitude turned the Civil Rights Bill into the Civil Rights Act of 1964.

But President Johnson used up some good will and prestige of the Presidency with his southern allies over that legislation. And he knew he would. He felt it was worth the price of handing the Democratic Party's South over to the Republicans to provide this improvement in the rights of Negroes.

By the time two years had passed it seemed like a long term. But the President, as much or more than I, did not want my departure to appear to be the result of industry pressure. Maybe it was silly to be concerned. Alan Boyd, a first-rate public servant who served as Chair of the Civil Aeronautics Board, Undersecretary of Transportation, and ultimately first Secretary of the new Department of Transportation, told me to ignore the industry's resignation drives. "They are like a pack of dogs nipping at your heels, Nick," he said. "They are going to keep it up all the time you're in office. One day you'll leave. And whenever it is, and whatever the reason, they'll cry out in unison, 'See, we got him!'"

President Johnson called me about 5:00 a.m. the day he was going to announce Alan Boyd's nomination as Secretary of Transportation. The President wanted to know what I thought of Boyd, whether he would make a good Secretary, and whether there was anything else the President should know about Boyd. I gave the President my approval for Boyd's nomination. It was a great example of the President's attention to detail, caution, and personal relationships. Why was he calling me, of all people? To get to my name on any list he must have made at least 100 phone calls to others.

About that time the *Washington Post*'s humor columnist, Art Buchwald, described the President's caution and preparations before declaring Mothers' Day. Buchwald wrote the President had called the equivalent of the congressional leadership, AFL-CIO President George Meany, and chair of the Joint Chiefs of Staff to find out the location of the Sixth Fleet before boldly announcing yes, America would again that year celebrate Mother's Day.

The President knew that I was (1) ready and willing to leave at any time, (2) grateful for the opportunity to serve, (3) anxious to get back to practice and then teaching, and (4) owed absolutely nothing by him, least of all another job. The weeks dragged by. Then, one lovely spring morning in 1966 I was summoned to the White House and ushered up to the family quarters.

Bill Moyers was talking to him while he shaved. A guard waited outside the bedroom. A band played in the Rose Garden, where a crowd gathered. Presumably the President was supposed to speak there at that moment.

He emerged from the bedroom, took me across the hall to a small dining room and ordered a cup of Sanka for both of us. He was relaxed and in good spirits. He thanked me for my work at the Maritime Administration, and said he understood I wanted to leave government. However, it was his view, shared by several advisors, that I should not be permitted to leave.

He then launched into a knowledgeable, detailed commentary about the impact of communications on our society including, among other things, the educational potential of broadcasting, a computer revolution, and prospects for communications satellites. He believed this was the most important area of our lives and our government, and he wanted me to serve as an FCC commissioner.

This created a problem. I'd really had enough of government. I was tired and wanted a return to law practice and teaching. The family was feeling the strain of my long hours and professional obligations. At the same time, given my upbringing it was difficult to say no to the request of any president – so long as it would not require anything immoral or illegal. Moreover, my relationship to President Johnson, along with his reputation for persuasiveness, made it impossible to say no to this president. Weighing it in the balance for a moment, I accepted.

Did the President know what he was doing? The speculation persists that he was surprised by my performance as a Federal Communications

Commissioner. I don't think so. He felt the pressure that flowed from my term as Maritime Administrator. He not only had the option, but my request to resign.

As the years wore on beyond 1968, and I became one of the very few Johnson appointees still in office, it seemed increasingly likely that I might be the last remaining bit of evidence that Lyndon Johnson did, after all, have a sense of humor.

Of course, he not only had a sense of humor, he also had a very lucrative television station in Austin, Texas. He was sensitive about it. Senator Barry Goldwater, his Republican opponent in the 1964 presidential campaign, was a private pilot. Goldwater was fond of saying he could always identify Austin, Texas, from the air because it was the only city in America of that size that had only one television tower. It was rumored that his position in the Senate (elected Majority Whip, 1951; Minority Leader, 1953) played a role in Lady Bird Johnson's acquisition of the KTBC-TV license in 1952.

I wasn't around then and don't know the facts. But many TV station licensees in the late 1940s and early 1950s, including in cities even larger than Austin, returned licenses to the FCC during those years when television's financial future looked bleak. It took a lot of money and business sense, or perhaps foolishness, to keep a television station license at that time. Lady Bird, often credited as the smarter business person of the two, ran a profitable radio station in Austin. And there didn't appear to be any competitors for the license when they got it.

The FCC established an allocations policy that gave a few TV stations high power and therefore extensive signal coverage, rather than many more low-power stations. Stations were clustered in large cities; in Texas this included Waco, San Antonio and Houston surrounding Austin. To avoid electronic interference the number of stations located in any geographical area is a function of their power, location, channel, and power of neighboring stations. The FCC may have been mistaken; America might have been better off with neighborhood TV stations. But it's unlikely those policies were adopted solely to give a Texas senator a television station monopoly in his hometown.

Whatever the facts may be, there was competition for KTBC-TV in Austin during my term on the FCC (1966-1973) from both over-the-air stations and cable TV. President Johnson has now died (January 22, 1973) and the station has been sold. But while he was President and I was on the Commission, he was extremely sensitive about any contact between him or his staff and anyone at the FCC.

Once he left the presidency we were free to reestablish communications. My last conversation was by phone, when he was in Acapulco and I wanted his best political judgment regarding the request of some Iowa Democrats that I run for U.S. Senate.

The independent regulatory commissions are sometimes called an arm of Congress; they are not executive branch agencies reporting to the president. President Johnson followed this understanding, this norm, and should be commended for doing so. But at least a portion of his motivation regarding the FCC, was his desire to avoid rumors he used untoward influence over an agency with regulatory responsibility for KTBC-TV, held in trust for him and his family.

After my FCC appointment was announced by the White House one of my first trips was a taxi ride from my Maritime office to the Commission. I had visited the FCC years before but couldn't remember where it was. Government agencies don't have street addresses, just zip codes: "Federal Communications Commission, Washington, D.C., 20554." That wasn't much help to a taxi driver who doesn't know the

building. A directory identified the location as "New Post Office Building," but still no street address.

I told the driver I wanted to go to the FCC. He didn't know where it was. "It's in the New Post Office Building," I replied, knowingly. "Mister," he shot back without turning around, "there ain't no New Post Office Building." He was right.

We ultimately found the building, a 1930s effort at 13th Street and Pennsylvania Avenue. FCC offices were in the attic. The spill-over was a couple blocks away, over a delicatessen on 12th Street.

The dingy yellow hallways had burned out lightbulbs and stacks of file boxes along the walls. It turned out the FCC has more cubic feet of paper per employee than any agency in Washington. The Commission's seal, a bird and some wires stretched between towers, did little more to suggest the world of television and communication satellites the President had told me about. Even then-Chairman Rosel Hyde, a kindly man not noted for his dry but well-hidden sense of humor, once wondered out loud whether the bird might be a carrier pigeon.

The late Len Weinles, an able public information officer whom I'd recruited in a nationwide search, couldn't stand the seal. But the legal hurdles to changing it were beyond the creative abilities of the FCC's lawyers. Len finally substituted an "fcc" logo of his own design one day, no one complained, and it remains the *de facto* official seal today.

Having found the building, I next went in search of Senator Warren G. Magnuson, Chairman of the Senate Commerce Committee. Chairman Magnuson's Committee had jurisdiction over the Maritime Administration as well as the FCC. He had taken the full force of the maritime industry's heat over my performance. "Do you think there will be any difficulty getting approval for the FCC nomination?" I asked. "Not over that appointment," he laughed. Apparently he assumed it impossible I could create more ire in the broadcasting industry than I had left behind in the shipping business.

The nomination was quickly approved, and the FCC borrowed a reception room from Postmaster General Larry O'Brien where my mentor, Justice Hugo Black, agreed to perform the swearing-in formalities. Because my father had died in the fall of 1965, at the age of 59, he was not present. As much as he and Mother enjoyed the Maritime Administration White House swearing-in, given Dad's professional career in general semantics and communications of another sort he would have taken special delight in the FCC appointment.

During June and July of 1966, the first two months, I attended the commissioners' meetings, carefully listened and observed, but did not actively participate except for an occasional question. While settling into a new office and recruiting staff it seemed best to show the deference to my colleagues appropriate for a young, inexperienced new commissioner.

There are seven commissioners, each appointed to a seven-year term, staggered to provide one appointment a year. If a commissioner leaves before his or her term expires the president can nominate a replacement commissioner to fill out the remainder of that commissioner's term.

E. William Henry had been Chairman of the FCC. He retired in May of 1966 after serving four years, leaving a three-year remainder to his term. Commissioner Rosel Hyde's seven-year term expired June 30, 1966. Thus, President Johnson had two positions to fill at the FCC. Rather than renewing Commissioner Hyde's service with another seven-year term as commissioner, the usual practice, he selected Hyde as Commission chair, gave me his seven-year term, and Hyde the remainder of Henry's term.

Former Chairman Henry's office was vacant. Unpretentious Rosel Hyde, entitled to it by right, did a quick benefit-cost analysis and concluded the benefit of a more prestigious and spacious office was outweighed by the burden of having to move. He didn't want it. Nor it turned out did any of the other commissioners, whose claims turned on their seniority on the Commission. So it fell to me.

Before I got there, however, most of the furniture had been stolen, or at least moved elsewhere. The standard executive furniture from the government's warehouse, the General Services Administration (GSA), is not only heavy, ugly and unimaginative, it is also very expensive. So, rather than order from GSA we worked with an able White House interior decorator. We ended up with a selection and arrangement that was bright and colorful, totally functional, very relaxed and warm, incredibly cheap, and totally out of character for the FCC. But at this point she could help me no more. The FCC procurement staff would have to place the order.

The comedy of errors which followed is worth a book of its own. The long and short of it was that it took months for the furniture to arrive, minor changes had to be redone numerous times despite the closest supervision, and several things were lost, including my diploma-sized official commission of office from the President, signed by Secretary of State Dean Rusk. An FCC employee took it to be framed and it was never seen again. If it was a plot to remove me from office it didn't work. Undersecretary of State George Ball later kindly signed a duplicate.

Much of what was accomplished during the FCC years must be credited to my exceptional staff. I brought with me from Maritime my first two assistants, both in their early twenties: Bob Thorpe and Mary Ann Tsucalas. Both stayed for the full seven and one-half years. Bob developed a popular following and strong professional reputation of his own in Washington, earned an M.A. in economics and law degree during that time, and is now associated with the prestigious Washington law firm Arnold & Porter. Mary Ann developed a reputation as one of the best office managers in government, married, and is still doing some freelance work. John Macy, Chairman of the Civil Service Commission, helped me find the very able and personable Doris Coles. When I left Commissioner Ben Hooks hired her, and she was still with the FCC as of this writing. A couple years later we acquired Bonnie Herbert from within the FCC for our permanent staff. Her ability earned her a position on Commissioner Glen Robinson's staff after I left. My first recruitment drive for a legal assistant produced Robert Bennett, a brilliant lawyer now a professor at Northwestern Law School in Evanston.

Justice William O. Douglas demonstrated the possibility of flexibility in staff so long as one stayed within budget. Because of his voluminous writing, instead of two law clerks he had one and used the additional money for secretaries. A quick story will illustrate.

In August of 1959, before Court opened in October, he was in the State of Washington Cascade Range, not just horseback riding, hiking and camping, but writing. Justices would often utilize, in varying degrees, their law clerks' initial evaluation of the thousands of petitions for *certiorari* (parties' requests the Court hear their appeal). Justice Douglas did his own. Regularly his clerk, Steve Duke, would receive packages from the Justice. The packages contained the Justice's notes evaluating the petitions, plus the manuscripts for three, that's right, three, books: a work on the Pacific Cascade (*My Wilderness: The Pacific West* (1960), as part of a multi-volume My Wilderness series), a child's biography of John Muir (*Muir of the Mountains* (1961)), and what I understood to be an academic study of the constitution of India (which may never have been finished and published, or may be his contribution to *In Search of India* (1960)).

My clerkship experiences with Judge Brown and Justice Black, for the traditional one year each, had been such that it seemed worthwhile to provide my own version of that experience to other young law graduates. Following Justice Douglas' example, I took the money other commissioners used to hire a relatively permanent engineering assistant and legal assistant and used it to hire two legal assistants for what were usually one-year terms. We also provided experience for summer interns, part-time volunteers, for-credit students, and seminar students. All told we gave over one hundred young people a taste of working in an FCC commissioner's office.

By the time Doris arrived, the office was still a shambles, but we had put together makeshift furniture in the legal assistant's office where I could sit to work. Since we still had no supplies Doris and I decided we would pay a visit to the keepers of the supply room. It proved to be not only a nice gesture toward some friendly employees seldom recognized by commissioners, but a revealing introduction to FCC management practices.

We began by asking for items sure to be on hand in any agency consuming as much paper as the FCC: paper clips and number two pencils. The FCC was out of paper clips and had been for some time we were told. Pencils? No one seemed to know where they were. Doris suggested we look in some metal cabinets. Her instincts were good but the supplies were incomplete. There were number one, three and four pencils, but no number two.

Upon inquiry it turned out they had never been instructed to maintain inventories or automatic ordering procedures and that they quite often ran out of stock. About three weeks later Commissioner Jerry Wadsworth stormed into a Commission meeting shouting at all of us, "Do you know we don't have any number two pencils in this agency?" "Yes," I said; "I know."

None of my colleagues either understood or thought much of my suggestion we adopt inventory control procedures, and so nothing was done. Later I discovered no one kept track of our franked (postage-free) envelopes either, and we apparently owed our landlord, Postmaster General O'Brien, $500,000 in back postage.

Inventory control was the least of the agency's problems. Its seeming unawareness of or hostility towards the most basic management procedures (recently studied and applied by us at Maritime) extended throughout the FCC. There was no management information reporting system, no statement of policy or goals, and therefore no identified way of measuring progress toward those goals. We didn't prepare and review a list of pending cases and certainly had no projected deadlines for their resolution. Fortunately, Senator Magnuson, seeing the need, asked for such a list. It was dutifully prepared and sent to him each year. Unfortunately, it was ignored by the commissioners.

We had no form of cost control. Cases, projects and studies were begun without any effort to estimate the employee hours necessary to complete them or the dollar value of any possible benefits. We had no personnel inventory of employees' skills, projected retirement dates and new recruitment needs. There was no effort to collect and routinely consider basic data and trends from the industries we were charged with regulating, including such basics as the number of TV receivers in the country.

There were no planning or special projects staff and offices or their equivalent. There was no internal auditor or inspector general. There was no personnel program worthy of the name. There was no chief scientist or office of science and technology to keep the Commission informed of new and future developments and their policy implications. The chief engineer's office performed unrelated line functions.

Computers had entered the commissioners' consciousness neither in terms of FCC use for routine processing tasks nor for their monumental implications for future national communication policies.

In short, the problem with the FCC's administration was not that it was administered badly, it was that it was not administered at all. An absence of administration necessarily comes to affect policy. But the Supreme Court isn't so brilliantly administered either and has no overall policy other than what's enunciated in its case-by-case opinions. Yet the Court seems to be able to resolve matters with a fair degree of analytical ability and an acceptable grasp of common sense and political reality.

Why not the FCC?

The answer lies in part in the intellectual quality of the commissioners and staff compared with that of the justices and their clerks, along with the comparative workloads and amount of research done within both institutions.

Let me make clear that lawyers and intellectuals are not the solution to government's problems. They have created many of those problems. Just as the Supreme Court would do a better job with greater diversity of all kinds – gender, geographical, racial, socio-economic, ethnic, and justices with experience as politicians and public officials – so does the FCC require more input from ordinary citizens. And not just input, but procedures for making that input influential. But the FCC is, above all, a policy-making institution. And for that task commissioners and staff with broad liberal arts education, ability to research, read, write, respect science and facts, and an ability to address issues without ideological or partisan biases is essential.

Unfortunately, there is even occasional evidence of anti-intellectualism. I once referred the resume of a Ph.D. in electrical engineering to the Chief Engineer. The response was not that the applicant was unacceptable or there were insufficient available positions. The rejection was that he was "too rich for our blood." Many of the FCC engineers were high school graduates who earned on-the-job credit as engineers during World War II. Few had engineering degrees so far as I knew. Given the relatively routine things they did that may not have been necessary. But somewhere in the FCC a trained scientist or engineer really could have helped.

Commissioner Lee Loevinger, previously a Minnesota Supreme Court judge and U.S. Department of Justice Assistant Attorney General Antitrust, currently practicing law in Washington, shared my felt need for more competent staff. We wanted a chief scientist and office of policy and planning. But the pressures of our colleagues' apprehension, antagonism and apathy ultimately wore us down.

The combination of industry influence from the subgovernment phenomenon, with the inability of the Commission and its staff to do independent analysis, coupled with their disinclination to accept help from others, produced disasters which varied only in their intensity, significance and humor.

Soon after our arrival at the Commission, one of the most significant and least humorous cases in FCC history came to the agency. It provided Bob Bennett, Doris Coles, Bob Thorpe, Mary Ann Tsucalas and me a year of intrigue and excitement before it was over. It was the effort by ITT, one of the nation's largest conglomerate corporations, to take over one of the three networks: ABC. Excerpts from one of my major dissents in that case comprise the next chapter. From it can be gathered a sense of my frustration over my colleagues' reaction to one of the most terrifying cases they were ever likely to encounter.

Chapter Six
The ABC-ITT Merger Dissent

Note: With one or two exceptions (e.g., Carterfone) the FCC opinions I wrote were concurring with or dissenting from those of the majority – a seven-year total of nearly 400. They are all currently available in volumes 4 to 44 of the Federal Communications Commission Reports, Second Series, available in hardcopy in some universities' law libraries, through proprietary online legal research services, and from my Web site https://www.nicholasjohnson.org (both in a list by year, and in full text). This chapter contains excerpts from one of those dissents. They are included because of the legal, economic, and media significance of the case, its illustration of corporate power, the attention it received at the time, and as an illustration of both what an opinion looks like and the proposition that sometimes the good guys do win.

After the dissenting opinions from two colleagues and myself the Department of Justice Antitrust Division got involved, and the FCC's approval of the merger was appealed to the U.S. Court of Appeals. Anticipating a probable loss, ITT dropped the case, ABC remained independent of the conglomerate, and the president of ABC, earlier required to advocate for the merger, privately thanked me for fighting it.

There were multiple opinions in this case. These excerpts are from the dissent in Application by ABC [ABC-ITT Merger], 7 F.C.C. 2d 245 (1966), beginning at p. 278. As with the text of this book generally, the language, facts and references in these excerpts have not been modified and should be read from the perspective of, in this case, 1966. Given the length of this opinion, for the benefit of researchers page numbers in the FCC Reports are indicated [in brackets] as are footnote calls; however, footnotes have been omitted from these excerpts. (Both page numbers and footnote calls are omitted from the much shorter opinions excerpted in subsequent chapters.)

Application by ABC [ABC-ITT Merger]
7 F.C.C. 2d 245, 278 (1966)
Dissenting Opinion of Commissioner Nicholas Johnson

[280] The Communications Act of 1934 vests this Commission with responsibility for evaluating, among other things, all proposed transfers of title to licensed broadcast properties. No broadcasting station license can be transferred, assigned, or disposed of without our permission. Our refusal prohibits the transfer. In passing upon applications for transfer the act provides that we must consider whether "the public interest, convenience, and necessity will be served thereby." [FN1] Unless we can make such a finding the application for transfer must be denied.

The present case, characterized as a merger of International Telephone & Telegraph Corp. (ITT) with the American Broadcasting Cos., Inc. (ABC), comes before us because of the transfer provisions of the act. Under the merger agreement ABC will transfer title of its 17 radio and television stations to an ITT subsidiary.

Ironically, the properties of greatest public significance, the ABC network and its affiliated stations, are not licensed property of ABC, and thus come within our jurisdiction only by virtue of their relation to the ABC-owned-and-licensed stations. [FN2] In order to approve the merger, the Commission must find that the transfer of the 17 ABC-owned stations to ITT will serve the public interest, convenience, and necessity. [FN3]

[281] A. THE MAJORITY'S PROCEDURAL APPROACH WOULD HAVE BEEN GENERALLY QUESTIONABLE IN ANY CASE, BUT HAS BEEN ESPECIALLY SO IN LIGHT OF THE SIGNIFICANCE OF THIS MERGER

It is deeply relevant to note at the outset that this particular transfer of broadcasting properties is the largest in history, and the largest this Commission is apt to encounter for some time to come. What is the Commission's role and responsibility in such a case? My disagreement with the majority over the answer to that question is far more

> *[T]he majority's treatment of this case, in my judgment, makes a mockery of the public responsibility of a regulatory commission that is perhaps unparalleled in the history of American administrative process.*

fundamental than any differences with regard to the merits. For the majority's treatment of this case, in my judgment, makes a mockery of the [282] public responsibility of a regulatory commission that is perhaps unparalleled in the history of American administrative process.

From the time the merger application was first filed, the outcome of this case has been a foregone conclusion. At one point no hearing at all was to be held. [FN4] Then, as a compromise to Commissioner Bartley's insistence on "a full evidentiary hearing," the Commission proposed an unprecedented, bobtailed "oral" hearing. [FN5] It was anticipated the Commission would merely meet informally *en banc* with the principals of ABC and ITT and hear their side of the case. Only the questioning of the three dissenting Commissioners extended the case to a scant 2 days. The questioning of 3 of the 4 Commissioners in the majority occupied scarcely 11 full pages in the 607-page record. [FN6] The fourth Commissioner's questioning was directed principally toward discrediting an FCC staff member and assisting ITT counsel's effort to demonstrate the absence of any possible antitrust implications of the merger. [FN7]

The most notable peculiarity of the "oral hearing" was the total absence of any party whatsoever representing the public. There were no intervenors. [FN8] (Indeed the absence of intervenors is sometimes read [283] by the Commission as evidence that the public interest coincides with the economic interest of the applicant. Needless to say, I do not abide such logic.) [FN9] More shocking, participation by FCC staff was barely evident. One employee of the Broadcast Bureau presented a very brief recitation of some issues that should be of relevance to the Commission. [FN10] Most had already been noted by Commissioner Bartley in his dissent to the "oral hearing" procedure. [FN11] There was no cross-examination by the staff of a single spokesman for the applicants. There were no witnesses whatsoever presented by the staff. The applicants came with able lawyers, economists, businessmen, and distinguished citizens. [FN12] The Commission had none.

To say that the individual Commissioners attended the hearing to represent the public is to totally miscomprehend the administrative process at this Commission. A Commissioner has but one legal and one engineering assistant. Between them they must pass upon a caseload that last year produced 3,030 pages of printed opinions, attend numerous meetings and hearings, and otherwise attend to the awesome business of Government involvement in this Nation's communications system – a system which includes, in addition to the American broadcasting industry, such matters as telephones, satellites, microwave, and mobile radio. [FN13] ITT and ABC combine financial resources represented by total revenues well in excess of $2 billion annually. [FN14] It [284] is questionable whether the entire staff of the FCC (with annual budget of $17 million) [FN15] would be adequate to deal with such corporations, even if engaged in nothing else. Clearly a single Commissioner's office is not. For that reason I make no representation that this opinion, and my own role in the hearing, are in any way adequate to serve the substantial public interest involved in this case. [FN16]

After the hearing things only got worse. I disclose no confidences when I say there has been considerable urgency within the Commission associated with the disposition of this case. There have been numerous references in the trade press to the fact that a substantial minority of this Commission has been fully prepared to decide the case without even waiting to hear from the Assistant Attorney General (Antitrust). [FN17]

Assistant Attorney General Donald F. Turner wrote FCC Chairman Rosel H. Hyde on November 3, 1966, that:

> Our analysis to date now indicates a sufficient possibility of significant anticompetitive effects to indicate that substantial antitrust questions are present. [FN18]

Only last evening (December 20, 1966) he advised us once again by letter that,

> we believe the possibilities of adverse effects are significant enough that we should call them to your attention, and that they deserve full and serious consideration by the Commission in making its determination whether, in light of these and other pertinent factors, the acquisition of ABC by ITT would serve "the public interest, convenience, and necessity." [FN19]

Turner's five-page single-spaced letter thoughtfully presents facts and analyses substantially at variance with the evidence presented to this Commission and, if true, leaves the majority's opinion in shreds. [FN20] [285] I am simply stunned and bewildered that the majority of this Commission could receive such a letter after 6 p.m. one evening and resolve a case of this magnitude before 10 a.m. the next morning.

I would think it appropriate to at least read Turner's letter slowly. Having done so, it seems to me essential that this Commission consider the information the Department of Justice apparently has available to it. Obviously, the majority has prevented that possibility. ... [FN21] Matters raised by the Department of Justice were not the only areas where information was clearly lacking. After cursory investigation it became obvious that the record was woefully inadequate with regard to ITT's foreign operations. [FN22] When it was suggested that the Commission might write the applicants for additional information, the present majority actually refused to sign the letter which was sent. [FN23]

Substantial quantities of information were filed in response (although partly evasive of the questions asked). [FN24] Again questions were posed (again over the majority's abstention), [FN25] and again quantities of information were supplied. [FN26] None of us has had adequate opportunity to consider this bulky material – most recently received on December 8, 1966 – any more thoroughly than the issues underlying last evening's letter from the Assistant Attorney General.

Why this rush? Surely it is praiseworthy for an agency to attempt to dispose of its workload expeditiously, especially an agency that is [286] repeatedly cited as an example of delay and indecision. [FN27] No one would defend processing cases for 5 and 10 years, though examples of such abound at the FCC. [FN28; "A particularly ironic example is involved in this very case. Hubbard Broadcasting has been seeking a clarification of the rights of its Albuquerque station, KOB, with regard to 770 kc, the frequency on which WABC in New York operates. For 20 years it has persisted. It still does not receive satisfaction in the majority's opinion.] But on what grounds can one charge delay by such an agency for taking more than 90 days to dispose of the largest case in its history?

And now the majority's opinion is bathed in public light. Reading it one is prompted to ask if those four Commissioners even believe the merits relevant to their decision. ... I make no brief for the analysis I have attempted to provide in this dissenting opinion. But at least I have attempted to identify issues and bring some rational analysis to bear. The Commission's opinion seems to me to have forsaken any such attempt.

The majority appears to be saying that a merger serves the public interest unless individual commissioners are willing and able to bear the burden of coming forward with evidence, and proof, that it does not. (Indeed, on occasion during the hearing, the applicants were almost hostile in their suggestion that commissioners were acting with impropriety in even questioning the public benefits from the merger unless armed with proof that potential evil would become reality.) [FN29] The majority appears to believe that some disservice to the public interest can be tolerated if it is not too severe.

Let me simply note briefly my disagreement with such propositions, for within these differences may lie some basis for logical understanding of the very wide variance between my approach and that of the majority.

Congress has provided that, "No ... station license ... shall be transferred ... except ... upon [a] finding by the Commission that the public interest, convenience, and necessity will be served thereby." [FN30] I believe such language contemplates that some transfers would not serve the public interest. I believe such language presumes that this Commission must seek and examine evidence that the public interest will be served by a given transfer. I believe the burden of coming forward with such evidence is on the applicants. I believe the burden of proof is on the applicants. I believe that without such evidence a proposed merger must be disapproved. I believe credible [287] evidence of probability that the public interest will be disserved by a merger precludes our finding that it serves the public interest.

If these assumptions be accepted, then the dissent which follows flows logically. If they be rejected, much of my opinion falls. In it the following arguments, here summarized, are expounded and documented at greater length.

B. THE MAJORITY'S SUBSTANTIVE ANALYSIS FAILS TO TAKE ACCOUNT OF THE ABSENCE OF EVIDENCE TO SUPPORT THE APPLICANTS' CASE, AND THE SUBSTANTIAL EVIDENCE OF PROBABLE HARM TO THE PUBLIC INTEREST

The merger was conceived in pursuit of personal and corporate interests wholly unrelated to the public interest. [FN31] ABC President Goldenson wished to retain control of a corporation threatened by a dissident minority. The value of his personal stockholdings has increased by about $3 million since the merger was announced. [FN32] ITT President Geneen sought to promote further growth through acquisition, and favored American corporations over foreign because of the present foreign-American balance in ITT's holdings. Prior to its merger with ABC 60 percent of ITT's income was from foreign sources. [FN33] ABC will be one of ITT's largest subsidiaries. [FN34] Such motivations are, of course, not necessarily inconsistent with serving the public interest in American broadcasting. But this explanation certainly puts the case for "the public interest" in unique perspective. And presumably no one would contend that these reasons, taken alone, are adequate to sustain the majority's approval of the merger.

> *[The merger] will place one of the largest purveyors of news and opinion in America under the control of one of the largest conglomerate corporations in the world. [T]hat the integrity of the news judgment of ABC would be affected by the economic interests of ITT is a real threat. ITT's economic interests are daily affected by what American citizens know.*

The public interest in broadcasting will be significantly harmed by the merger. It will place one of the largest purveyors of news and opinion in America under the control of one of the largest conglomerate corporations in the world, a company that derives 60 percent of its earnings from foreign sources and 40 percent of its domestic income from defense and space contracts. [FN35] The possibility that the integrity of the news judgment of ABC would be affected by the economic interests of ITT is a real threat, without regard to the character of the present management of ITT and ABC and their protestations that no possibility of harm exists. ITT's economic interests are daily affected by what American citizens know and think about what is going on in their country and the world. Moreover, to permit ITT to take over ABC tends to inhibit competitive forces in the broadcasting business. [FN36] It permits self-serving understandings between ITT's subsidiaries and ABC's advertisers. [FN37] It removes ITT as a [288] potential owner of a new network or broadcast properties not associated with a network. It makes it more difficult for a fourth network to come into existence. It tends to remove ABC as a party of protest to the international communication common carrier rates charged by ITT.

These reasons, standing alone, should leave little doubt in anyone's mind that the merger should not receive a blithe imprimatur from this Commission.

But there is another side to this case. The parties' side. What have ITT and ABC argued in support of the "public interest" served by the merger? Does it make sense?

The principal argument of the applicants, and the majority, is that the merger will permit ABC to become a stronger, more competitive network. [FN38] Each proposition advanced in support of this argument, however, simply fails to withstand analysis. ABC is substantially competitive with the other two major networks today. To the extent it is not, the evidence supports the view that the public is benefited by ABC's more innovative programming, not harmed. Certainly no one offered any evidence that ABC's programming is inferior to that of CBS and NBC – quite the contrary. The company is in good shape financially. Its earnings continue to increase. It has plans for expansion – made before proposal of the merger, and perfectly capable of execution without assistance from ITT. Moreover, ITT has made no specific commitment of funds to ABC. Indeed, Turner has advised the Commission that,

> ITT's estimates indicate that ABC's earnings growth rate over the next 5 years would be 16 percent. More importantly, it was anticipated that after capital expenditures and debt repayment, and assuming ABC continues in third place, it would yield a cash flow approaching $100 million between 1966 and 1970, almost all of which was thought by ITT to be available for reinvestment outside the television business. [FN39]
>
> But most fundamental is that, to the extent ABC is not fully competitive, the reasons lie wholly in the number and competitive position of its affiliated stations. The merger

can in no way affect that fact. The growth of UHF television can – and will.

Thus, even ignoring the substantial public detriment that will be caused by this merger, the Commission is not warranted in approving it in my judgment. The applicants have simply failed in sustaining their burden of proving that at least some public benefit will be derived from their merger.

And so I am brought to the substance of my dissent. But before I begin my analysis of the merits I wish to add one final word. That feelings about this case run high is obvious – and irrelevant to my evaluation of the issues. I think highly of both Geneen and Goldenson, the presidents of ITT and ABC. Each has rightfully made a reputation for himself as one of the ablest men in American business today. We are fortunate to have them. I think it probable America would be more benefited from their continued individual than from their new-found collective talents. We shall see.

[289] II. THE PARTIES SEEK TO MERGE FOR SELF-SERVING ECONOMIC AND PERSONAL REASONS UNRELATED TO SERVING THE PUBLIC INTEREST IN BROADCASTING

International Telephone & Telegraph Corp. is a sprawling international conglomerate of 433 separate boards of directors. [FN40] Its 1965 revenues of $1,782,939,000 make it 30th of the industrial corporations of the United States. Its net

> *ITT is a sprawling international conglomerate of 433 separate boards of directors.*

income that year was $76,110,000. [FN41] Its 200,000 employees – over 130 times the size of the entire Federal Communications Commission's Washington and field staff – make it fifth among U.S. industrial corporations and ninth in the world in size of work force. [FN42] ITT has significant holdings in at least 40 countries [FN43] and derives approximately 60 percent of its revenues from foreign sources. [FN44] It owns and operates the telephone companies in all of Chile, Puerto Rico, and the Virgin Islands, and in Lima, Peru, and the state of Parana, Brazil. [FN45] A great part of its foreign income comes from the sale of electronic and telecommunication equipment to foreign governments. [FN46]

Forty percent of ITT's U.S. revenues derives from Federal Government defense and space contracts. [FN47] But ITT also owns several consumer finance companies, life insurance companies, an investment fund, a small loan company, and numerous electronics research and manufacturing subsidiaries. [FN48] As a leading international common carrier, the company owns 10.5 percent of the shares of the Communications Satellite Corp. [FN49] (making it the second largest shareholder after the American Telephone & Telegraph Co.), and it elects two of the Comsat directors. ITT owns ITT Avis, Inc. (a car rental company), [FN50] and has acquired a sizable book publisher. [FN51]

The American Broadcasting Co., Inc., was literally born of this Commission's concern for "the fuller use of the radio as a mechanism of free speech." [FN52] The Radio Corp. of America (RCA) had owned two networks, the Red and the Blue. As a result of the FCC's chain broadcasting rules of 1941, the Blue Network Co., created by the National Broadcasting Co. (NBC) in 1927, was offered for sale. [FN53] It was purchased by Edward J. Noble in 1943 for $8 million, and Noble's "American Broadcasting Co." began. [FN54]

...

[290] ABC now owns 399 theaters in 34 States, 5 television stations, 6 AM and 6 FM stations (all in the top 10 broadcasting markets) and, of course, 1 of the 3 major television networks and 1 of the 4 major radio networks in the country. [FN58]

> *[With] its 137 primary television affiliates, ABC is capable of beaming [a] message to 93 percent of the 50 million television homes [and] 97 percent of the 55 million homes with radio receivers.*

Today with its domestic television network facilities and its 137 primary television affiliates, ABC is capable of beaming an aural and visual message to 93 percent of the 50 million television homes in this country. Its radio network can reach 97 percent of the 55 million homes in the United States with radio receivers. [FN59]

ABC's broadcasting and programming interests are not limited to this country. It has a wholly owned subsidiary which acts as program purchasing and sales representative for foreign stations. ABC has interests and associations with stations in 25 nations, known as the "Worldvision Group," including 11 Latin American countries, Australia, Canada, Japan, Lebanon, the Netherlands, Okinawa, and the Philippines. [FN60] A wholly owned subsidiary of ABC, ABC Films, distributes filmed television programs to stations, networks, and advertisers on a local, regional, or national basis, and abroad. [FN61]

ABC is in the record business, in the United States and abroad, through its wholly owned subsidiary ABC-Paramount Records. After all the subsidiaries are accounted for there are six labels (Command, Grand Award, Impulse!, Music Guild, Westminster, and White-hall), a record distributor, a recording studio, a record pressing plant, and music publishers. [FN62]

[291] Subsidiaries of ABC publish 3 farm papers, each over 100 years old, with combined circulation of 800,000: Prairie Farmer (Chicago), Wallace's Farmer (Des Moines), and Wisconsin Agriculturist (Racine). [FN63]

In 1965 ABC had total revenue of $476,500,000, of which $361,600,000 came from broadcasting. Its total before-tax net income for 1965 was $28,900,000, up from $22,200,000 in 1964. [FN64]

These are capsule descriptions of the breadth of interests encompassed in the two parent companies which come before this Commission seeking approval for their merger. [FN65]

It should not be surprising that the parties reached a decision to merge based on their own private interests. Serving their own interests is by no means inconsistent with their also serving the public interest. But the burden of establishing that what serves their own interest will also serve the public interest is obviously placed on the parties by the Communications Act. [FN66]

There is a history to the merger proposal which goes a long way toward explaining the private interests which the parties are attempting to serve. It provides a valuable perspective with which to view both the proposed merger and the claims made to the Commission by the parties. [FN67]

Since its inception about 45 years ago ITT has been largely a holding company for foreign telephone equipment and operating companies. [FN68] In 1959 Harold Geneen was selected as president by the ITT Board. Geneen immediately launched the company on a policy of growth, principally through acquisition, with the stated goal of doubling sales and earnings within 5 years. That goal was reached, and the policy of growth through acquisition has continued unabated. There can be little doubt that the success of the policy has been due largely to the personal qualities of Geneen. He "eliminated much of the autonomy of ITT's operating managers, and replaced it with a control system tautly run from New York headquarters." [FN69]

One of the aims of ITT's acquisition policy has been to redress the imbalance in its income from foreign and domestic earnings. [FN70] Thus, many of the acquisitions since Geneen became president have been U.S. companies. [FN71] The proposed merger with ABC is simply the latest and most ambitious of such purchases.

[292] ABC's merger-mindedness has an even more interesting history. In March 1964 it was reported that Norton Simon, prominent industrialist and art

collector, had acquired control of 100,000 shares of ABC stock. [FN72] Simon was reportedly interested in a seat on the ABC Board of Directors, but Goldenson, president of ABC, was opposed to any such ambitions of Simon. [FN73]

...

[293] The merger agreement provided for continuation of the ABC management and board, but dissident ABC shareholders found their influence was to be greatly diluted as holders of small proportions of the stock in a much larger company. That ABC's management viewed the merger at least partially as a defense against dissident stockholders became clear during the hearing before the Commission. In answer to whether the stockholdings of Simon accelerated ABC's interest in merger with ITT, Goldenson said, "Not Simon specifically, but any minority stockholder who would try to take a position to place pressures upon us." [FN79]

Thus did the expansion-minded conglomerate and the shareholder-shy entertainment complex find their way to this Commission, seeking approval of their proposed merger. This brief history of press comment on the events leading up to the merger becomes all the more interesting in light of the strained case which the parties made in attempting to justify their union as promoting the public interest.

[293] III. THE MERGER SUBSTANTIALLY HARMS THE PUBLIC'S INTEREST IN INDEPENDENT IMPARTIAL SOURCES OF INFORMATION, AND IN ECONOMIC COMPETITION

A. ITT'S FOREIGN AND DEFENSE INTERESTS ARE POTENTIALLY INCONSISTENT WITH THE INTEGRITY OF ABC'S NEWS REPORTING

The principal danger which inheres in this merger is not difficult to comprehend. Even the majority recognizes it. [FN80] It is the potential conflict of interest between the business interests which comprise ITT and ABC's broadcasting responsibility to the public, especially in news and public affairs.

...

[298] The number of potential conflicts is endless. One extreme but not implausible additional example might be offered. A dissident rebel movement could develop in a country where ITT had large investments. Brazil is the scene of recurrent anti-government agitation, [FN104] and ITT is heavily engaged in that country. [FN105] Suppose ABC news wished to produce a documentary picturing the rebellion as justified, and the government of Brazil insisted that the program not be shown? Would anyone in ABC news be inclined or feel free to propose the show in the first place? Would they be able to withstand suggestions from within or without ITT that ABC news' resources might better be used on other assignments? [FN106] The added leverage which the government of Brazil could exert because of ITT's Brazilian holdings would be substantial.

If such a situation seems unlikely, one need only think of the boycotts by Arab countries of companies which do business with Israel. [FN107] In Spain, where ITT has very large holdings, [FN108] the government has been boycotting a motion picture company since

1964 because one of its movies, "Ride a Pale Horse," dealt with the Spanish Civil War in a manner displeasing to the government. [FN109]

With all the inherent difficulties in obtaining accurate information from abroad, why risk even the remote possibility that news judgments presented to the American people might be distorted to serve ulterior corporate economic interests? What conceivable justification could there be for our government's participation (through today's action by this Commission) in the creation of a corporation that constantly will be confronted with a conflict between its own best economic interests and the needs of our people, and our government, for broadcasting [299] journalism of completely unimpeachable integrity from around the world?

Foreign relations provide a dramatic but by no means exclusive source of conflict between ITT's business interests and its duties as a broadcaster.

ABC might want to run a documentary favoring the use of domestic satellites for broadcasting. (Indeed, it happens to have been ABC that first proposed such a use, leading to the FCC hearing that produced the now famous Ford Foundation proposal for financing educational television with the money saved by broadcasting via satellite.) [FN110] ITT might have opposed this proposal because of its interest in the Communications Satellite Corp.

ABC might want to criticize the high level of defense spending, or the large sums being expended in the space effort, or even present programs which discuss conflicting views. [FN111] Because of ITT's interest in both defense and space work, such positions would jeopardize ITT's economic interests.

ABC might editorially favor truth-in-lending legislation, while ITT finance subsidiaries [FN112] would presumably be opposed.

In these and countless other ways ITT, as the owner of ABC, constantly will be faced with the conflict between its profit-maximizing goals – indeed, obligations to shareholders – which characterize all business corporations, and the duty to serve the public with free and unprejudiced news and public affairs programming. [FN113] The issue is both whether anything damaging to ITT's interests is ever broadcast, as well as how it is presented.

[300] History is not without examples of an obvious truth: Broadcast properties, like all other enterprises, sometimes will be used to serve ulterior ends when the opportunity arises. There are many examples – the following two are but illustrative: (1) Officials of the Trujillo regime in the Dominican Republic were reported to have paid $750,000 to officers of the Mutual Radio Network in 1959 to gain favorable propaganda disguised as news. [FN114] (2) Philco alleged to this Commission that RCA was using NBC stations to serve its broader corporate interests. In particular, (a) NBC stations said "a service of RCA" during station breaks; (b) NBC stations covered RCA activities as news when other stations did not; (c) color programs on NBC advised the public that RCA is the pioneer and developer of compatible color; (d) the "Today" show emphasized its origination in RCA

exhibition hall; and (e) NBC stations incorporated RC and RCA into their call letters. [FN115]

[301] Of course, there are many threats to news integrity beyond the kind of conglomerate takeover proposed by ITT. ABC has other, potentially conflicting, business interests of its own. [FN116] The influence of advertisers on program content has been often documented. [FN117] The "social control" of newsmen's independence has been studied. [FN118] The sociological pressures on management have been the subject of substantial theorizing. [FN119] The bias, or "credibility quotient," of the individual reporter is an important determinant of news accuracy. [FN120] No, [302] I would not suggest for a moment that conglomerate ownership is the only distorting lens between the space-time events of the real world and the reports that reach our citizenry. The entire process is worthy of diagnosis and treatment. But the evils of conglomerate ownership, like preventable disease, are unnecessary. The other factors are more difficult, perhaps impossible, to control. In any event, it is the issue of conglomerate control that is before us now.

The best we can do is to try to provide as much insulation as possible for the industry's programming from extraneous economic considerations. The worst we can do is to encourage mergers like this, which expose businessmen to the daily temptation to subvert the high purpose and indispensable role of the broadcast media in a free society.

...

If ITT is like most major corporations, it spends vast sums to influence its image and its economic relations – through advertising, [303] public relations, and Washington representation. [FN123] I am afraid I must concede that the assurances we have been provided – that ITT will be totally oblivious to the image created for it by its own mass media subsidiary, ABC – simply strain my credulity beyond the breaking point. Are we to accept, on the parties' own self-serving assurances, that although ITT may continue to exert pressure as an advertiser on the programming of CBS and NBC, it will exert none as an owner on the programming of ABC? Whether it be the product of realism or cynicism I simply must part company with what I believe to be the majority's naive and unreasoning faith in the parties' "express, positive, and binding representations as to future performance." [FN124]

It seems elementary to me that the only real way to find adequate safeguards for the public's interest in programming integrity is to give attention to the structure of the industry, not to assurances, albeit sincere, of interested parties who may be gone tomorrow.

...

[304] Rather than providing real safeguards, the majority points to unreal ones: "eternal vigilance ... continuing scrutiny for any indication that our reliance upon the assurances and safeguards set out on this record was not warranted." [FN126] How many times must it be pointed out that the kinds of decisions which this merger will encourage are not susceptible to scrutiny even by the most vigilant agency? And the Federal Communications Commission has a well-

earned reputation of being less than a thoroughly vigilant agency. [FN127] One recent incident involved the renewal of station licenses held by General Electric and Westinghouse. Officials of the two companies had been convicted of criminal violation of the antitrust laws. Section 313 of the Communications Act makes the antitrust laws specifically applicable to broadcast licensees and allows a court to revoke licenses even of civil violators. [FN128] And yet the FCC renewed GE's and Westinghouse's licenses without even holding a hearing. [FN129]

If the majority could point to any significant action which this Commission has taken in the past to assure the integrity of the news I might have greater faith in its "continuing scrutiny." In fact the examples are rare and trivial. There is neither monitoring nor preservation of the broadcasting product. Thus, the raw data does not even exist from which to determine how licensees treated subjects which affected their other business interests should some future "eternal vigilance" require such information. [FN130] Moreover, too close a scrutiny could be mistaken for censorship or intimidation, which our laws and Constitution forbid. [FN131] No, the only practical way to combat untoward use of broadcasting facilities by conglomerate corporate ownership is in providing the proper structure for the industry in the first place. When the majority rejects that truth it thereby effectively abdicates responsibility for this most "vital element of broadcast service." [FN132]

[305] B. THE MERGER DOES NOT BENEFIT ECONOMIC COMPETITION AND MAY SERVE AS A SIGNIFICANT DETERRENT

...

[No] one can question that the effect on competition in broadcasting and networking should be relevant to this Commission in determining whether to approve a transfer of broadcast properties.

Obviously, it cannot serve the public interest for this Commission to approve the merger if the two companies will thereby violate the antitrust laws. But our concern is not negative; it is not enough that the merger would not violate the antitrust laws. The standard is, or should be, affirmative. Will the merger promote competition, or otherwise serve the public interest? It is not our task to sue to dissolve merged companies that do not serve the public interest. That is the responsibility of the Department of Justice. Our job is to authorize the merger of none but those companies that will promote the public interest.

The proposed merger has been pictured both by the parties and by the majority as necessary to enhanced competition among the three networks. Little attention has been given to the detriment which might be worked by the merger on competition in the network market – the existing three-network market, and possible future markets with more competitors.

It is my view that the supposed benefits to competition are unreal or unfounded hopes, and that inhibition rather than enhancement of competition is likely to result from the merger. Indeed, in my opinion, the merger may well violate section 7 of the Clayton Act. [FN134]

...

[306] The television network market is confusing because we usually think of the viewer as the consumer and the program as the product. That is certainly the perspective of the regulator whose duty it is to see that the interest of the public – *i.e.*, the viewer – is served. But in an economic sense this is at best a shadow analysis. Whether or not, as [307] McLuhan tells us, the medium is the message, [FN138] the true consumer is the advertiser, and the true product the viewer. The advertiser pays for the viewers which the network can deliver. The program is but the vehicle for delivering viewers – potential purchasers of the advertiser's wares.

> *The television network market is confusing because we usually think of the viewer as the consumer and the program as the product. [T]he true consumer is the advertiser, and the true product the viewer. The program is but the vehicle for delivering viewers.*

...

[324] I believe the procedural and administrative process by which the Commission has resolved this case to be inadequate to the magnitude of the issues involved. I believe its inadequate and hasty handling of the case has – unnecessarily, and to some extent unjustifiably – created an appearance that has called into question the integrity of the Commission's process.

I believe these procedures have also adversely affected, in fact, the substance of the Commission's evaluation of this case.

We have just passed upon the largest transfer of broadcast properties in the history of the industry. We have done it without adequate information, without adequate articulation of the relevant public interest standards, without subjecting the allegations and reasoning of the applicants to the scrutiny of adversary process. Under these circumstances it is not surprising to me that the opinion of the majority leaves much to be desired.

...

This case involves the largest transfer of broadcast properties in the history of the world. It is probably the most important this Commission will confront in the foreseeable future. If my estimate is at all accurate, then the majority opinion is indeed a remarkable document. For the opinion stands as little more than an unconvincing rationalization for the quite inadequate procedures used in this case, which, to date, have unearthed facts clearly insufficient to justify the proposed merger.

...

[330] And so we come to the end of what has been for me an eventful introduction into the issues of broadcast ownership in America. If the merger is to come about I can only hope that the concerns I feel will prove groundless. But whether they do or not, I have no question that the exercise has been worthwhile. Many have participated in this case. Many more have and will reflect upon it. The experience cannot help but produce

a greater awareness on the part of all Americans of their responsibility for the integrity of the public's media in a society of free men.

Chapter Seven
Broadcasting Policy: The Bulls and the Blodgetts

The preceding chapter contains only excerpts from one dissent in one phase of a two-year proceeding that produced hundreds of pages of FCC opinions and thousands of pages of hearing record. ITT as a company and the ABC-ITT merger as a case have been written about at length by others (*e.g.*, former intern now Dr. Karen Possner). The excerpt in the previous chapter fails to include, among other things, the detailed description of the 433 corporations that made up ITT, or the way they conducted a foreign relations policy all their own – occasionally in violation of U.S. law. It does not repeat the shocking revelations of ITT's efforts to manipulate the media coverage of a subsequent phase of this very FCC proceeding – an evaluation of ITT's assurances that it would always respect ABC's journalistic independence and integrity.

This occurred before ITT's effort to prevent the nationalization of its Chilean telephone company. It included an offer of $400,000 to President Nixon and $1,000,000 to the CIA for influence with the Chilean government – an influence ultimately enabling the overthrow of that government and death of President Salvador Guillermo Allende.

All this and more has been omitted because this is a book about the FCC not ITT. (Readers interested in more about ITT will find the exploration fascinating.) The excerpts in the previous chapter are selected to illustrate the Commission's process in one of its largest and most significant cases. If the FCC would ever have wanted to do its very best, this would have been the case. Instead, it approached a case of the magnitude of ABC-ITT with a firm commitment to the corporations' wishes. With its lack of regard for rather obvious public interest considerations, with its seeming inability to apply the most elementary of rational analyses, one can fairly expect it to do little better with the routine cases.

Following the hearing in the spring of 1967, by which time many of the dissenters' suspicions had become proven facts, the majority again approved the merger. This time the Department of Justice was in the case, and filed an appeal with the U.S. Court of Appeals, District of Columbia. The case name said it all: *The United States versus Federal Communications Commission*. It seems to me a perfect way to express the Commission's relationship to the national interest. It was as if the whole country was suing the FCC – and in a sense it was.

My feelings about the FCC, the broadcasting industry, the threats and significance of corporate ownership of media would never be the same after this case. That appeared to be true for others who followed the proceeding, whether in government, the media, or the academic community.

It was also my introduction to "no-lose strategies." Our work on the ABC-ITT case had taken an enormous amount of time. And yet, in one sense, we had lost. The FCC approved the merger, not once but twice. It was ITT's giving up once the Antitrust Division took ITT to court, not our dissents, that prevented the merger. But in a broader sense we had won. We had gained a number of strategic advantages.

Meaningful reform requires the attention, education and participation of the American people – opinion leaders, public officials, media, academic community and citizenry. Certainly this was true of FCC reform. Like other agencies and regulatory commissions, its routine work received relatively little if any attention from those just mentioned. It might as well have been working under a rock. So long as that continued, the FCC and its supporting subgovernment were safe.

The capacity to offer public dissent to its actions, in relatively clear writing, changed all that. Education of the public regarding the outrageous performance of the FCC became a supplementary goal to the winning of individual cases.

Thus the "no-lose strategy." If a dissenting opinion could alter the opinions of the other commissioners, as it sometimes did, then an individual case was won. If it could not, and the majority's opinion went out in its original outlandish form, the dissent served to make Congress, media and public more aware of the need for investigation, reporting and reform of the FCC and its processes. Once the role of outnumbered, dissenting commissioners was perceived in this way the stress associated with each case vanished. We just took on the worst cases, tried to keep the workload within bounds, and went at it.

The power of a dissent in legal terms turns on whether there is anyone to appeal. When there was we developed a good record of court reversals of Commission majority opinions. The commissioners did not like to be reversed. When a court returned a case to the Commission the majority would often come to the same conclusion but rewrite its earlier opinion to make it more difficult to overturn. However, when there is no party to appeal commissioners are unconcerned about court review and dissenting opinions; they know the impact of dissents is limited to press reaction.

The Justice Department did appeal the ABC-ITT case. It was argued before the U.S. Court of Appeals for the District of Columbia. But during the first few days of January 1968, before the Court could issue its opinion, ITT called off the merger.

In a way, we had won. There was no merger. But it was a frustrating victory, an atypical case. There has not been another effort to take over a network during 1966 to 1975. There were other significant cases during my term, but none like ABC-ITT.

In another sense, however awful the FCC majority's handling of the ABC-ITT case was, it represented the FCC at its best. With the rare intervention by the Justice Department, extensive press coverage and dissenting opinions, the commissioners were putting forth their best possible arguments for approving the merger.

It was the smaller, routine cases that made up the bulk of the Commission's business. In total they constituted greater travesty. But how could we convey this fact? Many FCC watchers viewed ABC-ITT as an aberration. Once the merger was abandoned they assumed all was well at the Commission.

Watching the opinions flow by at the regular weekly Wednesday meetings was somewhat like watching the debris float down a polluted river during spring floods. One could not possibly fish out every piece of trash, position it on the river bank and write an essay about it. Given the Commission caseload we could not possibly write a separate opinion in every case. Occasionally I felt like we should select one week's agenda of cases and write a dissent covering all of them. Ultimately we did that in an article published in the *Yale Law Journal* (excerpts in Chapter Ten).

Meanwhile, we selected examples to highlight intellectual bankruptcy, failure to formulate national communications policy and follow precedent, club-like favoritism for largest licensees, and other grievances. After seven years-plus my office had produced 376 opinions discussing such examples, an average of about one a week.

The examples in this chapter are illustrative of the often-humorous lengths to which petty bureaucratic detail can carry an august body like the FCC. The first dissent involves the web of regulations the FCC has spun for itself and licensees and the resulting ensnarement created by the Commission's seeming inability to permit a station on a mountain to *say* it is on a mountain.

The second involves land mobile radio, such as radios in police cars and taxis. There are millions of such radios. Each licensee wants the best frequencies for their needs. The FCC decides who will, and won't, get them. There are logical approaches. Licensees could bid. The Commission could make economic analyses of the comparative cost effectiveness of competing uses. It could get out of this business, leaving it to the market and courts to work it out. Instead the FCC has defined its own categories of use, makes arbitrary choices among them, and then decides on the highest use when they conflict. The case illustrates what happens when a milk cow meets a bull.

The third case is not so funny. It is a routine application for an increase in power. So what? So your AM radio band becomes even more congested with interfering signals than now. How does it happen? One case at a time, none of which is individually very significant. This is an illustration.

The fourth and final case study reprints both the brief text of the Commission's opinion and my dissent in their entirety. Unlike the mountain case, it is a more typical example of the Commission's lenient enforcement of its regulations.

Application of Sierra-Pacific Radio Corp. (KOSO)
7 F.C.C. 2d 61, 62 (1967)
Dissenting opinion of Commissioner Nicholas Johnson

I dissent.

The Federal Communications Commission has today forbidden the location of a radio station on a mountain – Mount Oso, in California. Why? Because our rules require stations be located in communities, and, as everybody knows, an unpopulated mountain is just not a community.

There are apparently to be but two exceptions under the terms of the majority's opinion. (1) An unpopulated area can be a "community" if people reasonably can be expected to "spring up." (2) Mount Washington, in New Hampshire – the only unpopulated mountain "community" in the table of assignments ....

One would be reasonable in one's suspicion that this case must have threaded its way to us through a metaphysical morass of geography and bureaucracy. Especially is this so in view of the fact that KOSO's transmitter and antenna have, in fact, been physically situated on Mount Oso for some time, and its call letters rather prominently contain the letters "OSO."

> *The FCC has today forbidden the location of a radio station on a mountain – Mount Oso. Why? Because our rules require stations be located in communities, and, as everybody knows, an unpopulated mountain is just not a community.*

The FCC has taken advantage of the fact that words can mean what it wants them to in its electronic palace in wonderland. Thus, "location" has been defined as something having nothing to do with the geographical placement of a station's studio, transmitter, or antenna tower. Stations must broadcast their call letters and location. And "the station will be considered to be located in ... [the] community which will be specified in the station license." A station need not even have a studio in the community in which it is located. For, although a rule expressly provides that "each station shall maintain a studio, which shall be known as the main studio, in the place where the station is located," the same subsection contains its own built-in waiver: "Provided, That the main studio may be located at the transmitter site whether or not the transmitter site is in the place where the station is located."

The owners of station KOSO purchased the station when it was assigned to Turlock, Calif., and was being operated under the call letters KHOM. They subsequently sought and received this Commission's approval to move the station location to Patterson, Calif., and put the transmitting equipment on Mount Oso. This was approved because – although no station had been assigned to Patterson – our rules provide that, "A channel assigned to a community listed in the table of assignments [Turlock] is available upon application in any unlisted community [Patterson] which is located within 25 miles of the listed community." Patterson is but 15 miles from Turlock. Mount Oso, we have been informed, is approximately 28 miles from Turlock.

At first blush the uninitiated might think Mount Oso eliminated as a possible location for a station assigned to Turlock because it is 3 miles beyond the 25-mile limit. But, no. That geographical misfortune, like the thousands of other snares in the 1,681 pages of Commission rules, could be removed quite easily. Borrowing from the lore of magic wands we could just waive the rule – itself a waiver of the table of assignments to communities. Although the somewhat ambiguous and unarticulated criteria for rule waiver have not yet reached the conceptual intricacies of the early common law writs, their understanding and mastery are equally limited to specialists in the practice. In any event, the majority opinion indicates (though without apparent explanation) that the Commission would have been fully prepared to consider a waiver in this case. No, the problem lies not in Mount Oso's horizontal distance from Turlock, but in its vertical distance. For no interpretation of the Commission's rules can change the fact that Mount Oso, is, quite clearly and unmistakably, an unpopulated mountain.

It is not unnatural that a station owner might want to place his or her facilities on a mountain. A station located in a community often has its transmitter and antenna on the highest spot available simply because it increases its signal coverage area. What better high spot than a mountain? Moreover, mountains have always held a fascination for man. The majority apparently accepts the applicant's assertion in this case that Mount Oso – Spanish for the romantic mountain bear – is a "much better known, famous, and more prominent place" than either Turlock or Patterson, Calif.

It was Samuel Francis Smith who, in 1831, wrote the song that prompted all Americans thereafter to cry out,

From every mountain-side
Let freedom ring

And even if the last line has more recently come into prominence in telephonic communications, we can assume that the author of "America" would have no objection to our today applying the two lines to broadcasting from Mount Oso. It was long before the days of radio that Lord Byron sensed,

146 – Catfish Solution

High mountains are a feeling, but the hum
Of human cities torture

and, if even closer ties with modern-day broadcasting are required, that Walter Savage Landor wrote,

The mountains are our sponsors ....

What finer, more appropriate place for a radio station to be located than atop a mountain? How, then, could the majority have come to its conclusion?

We cannot be sure. The opinion gives little illumination – beyond its insistence upon the strict enforcement of past practice. We may safely assume, however, that its reasons lie somewhere in vaguely conceived notions of "local service" and "community identification." A radio station is supposed to

> **This Commission has evidenced almost no concern about the quantity and quality of local programming.**

provide local service. It can be located in any community up to 25 miles away, and have its transmitter, antenna, and studio on a mountain, and still provide the requisite local service. But once it identifies with the mountain for purposes of station identification – so the argument might run – hopes for local service will vanish.

There are two things wrong with this argument.

(1) This Commission has evidenced almost no concern about the quantity and quality of local programming. I am sure that it is partially as a consequence that many stations provide very little, if any, meaningful local service. Records, program

packages, network programming, and advertising are very largely indifferent to locality. In this instance, as the majority acknowledges, "KOSO is programmed as a 'good music' facility with a minimum of interruptions on the hour and half hour, and the programing thus appeals to a listening audience of far greater scope than the population of Patterson." What difference does it make, under these circumstances, where a station is located?

(2) If this Commission, or KOSO, were to believe that the station should provide a "community service" to those people living in the communities within its listening area, it easily could do so. Local news, sports, announcements of local events, interviews and public affairs programs, coverage of local events, etc., could be provided as well by a station identified with Mount Oso as with Patterson – a "city" of 2,246 people who are obviously but a small proportion of KOSO's total listening audience (within an area up to 85 miles from Patterson).

It is highly possible that a station which is not held responsible to serve as local outlet for any community may simply end up not being responsible, period. It would not have to make any announcements in any local area at renewal time. And its obligations to its listening public, insofar as serving local needs and interests are concerned, might become so diffuse as to vanish. In dissenting to the majority's resolution of the issues posed by this case, I do not mean to endorse the principle that a station should have no responsibility to serve the listeners within its signal area. It is just that, in my view, local service is independent of our extraordinarily complex rules regarding station location.

I am principally disturbed because, although the Commission goes to great length to require adherence to the rule here in question, it does not follow through with the much more important task of seeing to it that stations serve as outlets for local expression. To renew the licenses of stations which earn millions of dollars in advertising revenue and provide little or no meaningful local public service programming, while at the same time denying the present request because of some unarticulated pretense of desire for local service, makes little sense. For it is not the form, but the substance, against which our efforts to insure operation in the public interest must, and will, be judged.

I have written before of my concern for our failure carefully to think through what we are, and what we are not, doing in regard to local service. I need not repeat those analyses here. It does seem to me, however, that the Mount Oso case neatly exemplifies the lengths to which our present chaos has carried us. Even from this mountaintop I cannot see the end of the trail.

Petition of Lehigh Cooperative Farmers, Inc.
10 F.C.C. 2d 315, 317 (1967)
Dissenting Statement of Commissioner Johnson

The FCC has today found, in full and solemn formality, that "livestock breeding" is a higher use of mobile radio than "dairy inspection."

The case illustrates, beyond the wildest imaginings of comics and critics, the absurdity of our present procedures and standards for allocating mobile radio frequencies.

Lehigh Valley Cooperative – 2,400 dairy farmers in Pennsylvania, New Jersey, Delaware, and Maryland – is typical of the users of the 5 million transmitters now serving our over-growing industrial economy. It would like to operate a radio-controlled "dairy inspection service" with frequencies in the Special Industrial Radio Service – as it used to operate a radio-controlled "livestock breeding service."

Needless to say, we have regulations covering this matter. Section 91.501(d)(3) of our rules provides livestock breeding is an "eligible activity" for the Special Industrial Radio Service Frequencies. There is no provision in the rules for a "dairy inspection service."

> **The FCC has today found, in full and solemn formality, that "livestock breeding" is a higher use of mobile radio than "dairy inspection."**

Accordingly, we suggest the applicant use the much more congested Business Radio Service.

What is the difference between these two activities?

Our opinion states that a "dairy inspection service" consists of "unannounced inspection of a member's total operation," and "periodic and immediate inspections" of "milk before it is loaded in tank trucks," and "a member's entire operation in the event that mastitis (inflammation of the mammary glands) is discovered in the morning milk." The opinion then, with beguiling delicacy, if ambiguity, leaves entirely to the reader's active urban imagination the details of the operation of a radio-controlled "livestock breeding service." "Call bulls," perhaps? Whatever the details, it is difficult for me to find the latter a "higher use" than the former and I would, therefore, grant the application.

I would also urge, once again, that we get on with the increasingly urgent business of formulating a rational and effective means for allocating frequencies among competing users, whether on economic or other grounds.

Application of Storer Broadcasting Co.
12 F.C.C. 2d 282, 285 (1968)
Dissenting Opinion of Commissioner Nicholas Johnson

The two AM radio stations involved in this case, WTOP and WJBK, operate on 1500 kc [kilocycles]. WTOP is in Washington, D.C.; WJBK is in Detroit. WJBK wants to put out a more powerful signal at night – an increase from 1,000 w [watts] to 5,000 w. WTOP (which now operates with 50 kw

> *It seems to me we need go no further than to listen to our own home and automobile AM radios at night. The overlapping signals and congestion are a monument to years of decisions like this one.*

[kilowatts; 50,000 watts] at night) says WJBK's increase in power will cause more interference to WTOP's nighttime signal.

I will not attempt a detailed discussion of the engineering data and procedures involved in a case of this kind. It seems to me we need go no further than to listen to our own home and automobile AM radios at night. The overlapping signals and congestion are a monument to years of decisions like this one – our definitions of "acceptable interference"; rules that permit interference in the name of "a first service" for a community that may well be a suburb of a metropolitan area with multiple stations; shoehorned stations with "directional" antenna patterns; bootstrapped automatic increases in power once a 250-watt daytime station is established; the very definitions of "daytime"; and then the "waiver" or liberal interpretation of the rules that do exist.

The Commission makes a creative, and in many instances commendable, effort to satisfy as many requests as possible. The danger, of course, is that our efforts to serve everyone may end up serving no one. And the ultimate irony is that, when substantial numbers of listeners finally give up, and go from AM to FM listening, the very owners creating the signal interference today will be the ones to suffer the greatest financial loss tomorrow.

I would prefer stricter engineering standards and a higher burden of proving noninterference by those who seek to increase power than the Commission applies in this case and, accordingly, dissent.

Application of Esther Blodgett
14 F.C.C. 2d 342 (1968)

Dissenting Opinion of Commissioner Nicholas Johnson

Before us today is the saga of an 11-year battle of wits between this 34-year-old federal bureaucratic institution and a wily septuagenarian woman born and raised in the heartland of the Midwest. Judging from the conclusion reached by the majority today, the woman appears to have won.

> *Before us today is the saga of an 11-year battle of wits between this 34-year-old federal bureaucratic institution and a wily septuagenarian woman born and raised in the heartland of the Midwest. [T]he woman appears to have won.*

I believe that this story is worth telling in some detail. Its lessons are important both to an understanding of the power of an individual in an age of seemingly overpowering institutions, and to an understanding of the workings of the FCC.

The tale begins in an improbable village known as Harvard, Ill. At last count, Harvard boasted a population of 5,019. Located just an LP's toss from the Wisconsin State line, Harvard lies in the epicenter of our Nation's milk cow country.

In February 1955, radio station WMCW (which, its letterhead explains, is short for the "Milk Capital of the World") first took to the air, under the ownership and direct supervision of station manager Esther Blodgett. Miss Blodgett is a lifetime resident of the greater

Harvard area, but, as subsequent events demonstrate, decidedly worldly in the ways of Washington, D.C.

Difficulties with Miss Blodgett first began in 1956, when she filed with the Commission an application for renewal of WMCW's license. The Commission staff noted the application was incomplete, and deferred action. After further correspondence, Miss Blodgett completed the application and the Commission elected to renew her license for a full 3-year term.

In 1959, the Commission was forced once again to defer action on a WMCW renewal. This time Miss Blodgett neglected to file the application until after her license had expired. When the application did arrive it was, once again, incomplete. The Commission again asked Miss Blodgett to complete the application form, and, later, again elected to renew the license, although for the limited period of 1 year.

In 1961, Miss Blodgett maintained her superb batting average by being deferred for a third time in the face of an impressive list of multifarious violations, such as:

Failure to file her renewal application until WMCW's license had expired;

Failure to comply with the publication requirements of section 1.359;

Failure to file a complete application;

Failure to file financial reports for the previous 2 years;

Failure to file an ownership report; and

Failure to adequately explain certain violations listed in an official notice of violation issued in November 1964.

For reasons which remain enigmatic, the 1961 deferral was permitted to drag on until 1966, when we again relented and granted WMCW a renewal for 1 year.

In each of these instances, the Commission was satisfied that a mild rebuke would be sufficient to impress Miss Blodgett with the seriousness of her cavalier attitude. But for all of our studied leniency, Miss Blodgett continues to plod along at her own chosen pace, filing requisite forms with the Commission whenever the fancy seems to strike her.

On June 10, 1967, this protracted Parkinsonian struggle between Miss Blodgett and the Federal Government reached a climax. On that date, the Commission mailed to Miss Blodgett an

> *Miss Blodgett continues to plod along at her own chosen pace, filing requisite forms with the Commission whenever the fancy seems to strike her.*

official notice of violation. By the terms of the notice, a reply was to be filed with the Commission within 10 days. Not having heard from Miss Blodgett within that time, we mailed to her an appropriate warning one month later. Still not having heard from her as the summer waned, we deferred action on WMCW's renewal for a fourth time on September 5, 1967.

[C. Northcote Parkinson's Law of Standard Deviation is explained as involving a known rate of ascension from the bottom to the top of the heap in bureaucratic "In" boxes. Thus, for example, if it is known that it takes

24 days for a letter to rise from the bottom to the top of the In box, a person seeking to avoid having the bureaucracy making any decision at all need only insure that a letter reaches that In box every 23 days. When a letter arrives, the appropriate file (now near the top of the heap) is returned to the bottom, to begin its ascent all over again. If carried on long enough, Dr. Parkinson assures us, the bureaucrat will never answer the first letter, since he or she will never see the file come to the top of the In box. Parkinson, *Parkinson's Law* (1957), pp. 99-100.]

Naturally, we were delighted to hear from Miss Blodgett eventually, even though nearly a year after our original notice of violation. In a letter received in May 1968, Miss Blodgett informed us that the violations initially complained of had been fully corrected.

Thus has ended, at least for the moment, the tale of Miss Esther Blodgett and her struggle against the formalities of the FCC. As the majority must recognize, this saga presents an extraordinary problem of constancy of the sort which would baffle even John Donne. ("Now thou hast lov'd me one whole day/Tomorrow when thou leav'st, what will thou say?" John Donne's "Woman's Constancy.") The Commission, in determining to assess Miss Blodgett a $500 forfeiture, manifests its hope that she will henceforth mend her unusual ways and display more respect for Commission regulations and diligence in replying to Commission inquiries. But it renews her three-year license.

I am not convinced, however, that Miss Blodgett's demonstrated indifference to this Commission will be altered by this action. It seems clear, in the first place, that the majority's decision only confirms what must have been suspected by Miss Blodgett all along: however long she waited to reply to a notice of violation the worst that could happen would be an increase in postal rates. In repeatedly confirming this notion, the Commission cannot express surprise that its licensees now respond, like the pigeons of B. F. Skinner, to the behavior it rewards. By winking at such behavior the Commission also lends credence to a gathering

> *[T]he majority's decision only confirms what must have been suspected by Miss Blodgett all along: however long she waited to reply to a notice of violation the worst that could happen would be an increase in postal rates.*

crescendo of complaints which broadly charge that this Commission applies a dual standard: a jaundiced eye and letter-of-the-law punctiliousness so far as activities of members of the public seeking to participate in Commission proceedings are concerned, while springing to the defense of broadcasters who openly transgress the plain mandates of the rules.

In the second place, I am disturbed by the Commission's reluctance to hold a hearing into the reasons for this history of phlegmatic correspondence. We know too little about the circumstances which may have compelled Miss Blodgett's procrastination. If, as the evidence suggests, Miss Blodgett is at once station manager, announcer, advertising agent, secretary, and owner of an unprofitable WMCW, then this Commission may want to make allowances for the frail position of such a meagerly financed station. In this light, the standard forfeiture imposed would appear to be too drastic an action.

On the other hand, it may be, as the evidence is equally suggestive, that Miss Blodgett is simply lackadaisical by nature, or even downright obstinate. In that event, a mere forfeiture, hand-in-hand with a full-term renewal, does not go far enough.

In either event, it is my view that interested members of the public should be given the opportunity to inform the Commission's judgment. We have been informally apprised by the FCC staff that WMCW's programing reflects conscientious attention to local needs and interests. We understand, too, that the community has repeatedly expressed its deep appreciation to Miss Blodgett for her efforts at WMCW – an appreciation luncheon having once coincidentally occurred on the very day an official FCC communication was received. Such admirable policies and community support should be encouraged by the Commission. A hearing in the Harvard community could uncover such evidence.

Perhaps the Commission's rules should be changed in some respects that affect licensees like Miss Blodgett. In the meantime we simply must insist that all licensees obey the Commission's rules. It has been charged, with some justification, that the

Commission is all too ready to enforce its rules against small broadcasters, and equally too willing to overlook infractions by corporate-owned stations. In my judgment, the best way to eliminate such practices and dispel suspicions is to make it our practice to insist on hearings in all renewal cases where issues like this arise.

Accordingly, I dissent.

These are but four examples of a more typical FCC workload than the rare ABC-ITT monster case. The FCC's primary impact comes from the cases that come from Detroit, Michigan, Patterson, California, Harvard, Illinois, and the land mobile needs of mid-Atlantic dairy farmers. Multiply these four cases by a thousand and you'll have a better sense of what the FCC is up to.

Chapter Eight
FCC Programming Regulation: Seven Years of Hyde and Seek

However murky the FCC's procedures and decisions may be, it is very clear what it is not doing. It is not regulating the programming performance of its licensees.

There are some 8,000 radio and television stations in the United States. Each holds a license from the FCC. Those licenses entitle the licensee to broadcast for a three-year term, at the end of which the license must be renewed. As the opening section of the Communications Act puts it:

> It is the purpose of this chapter, among other things, to maintain the control of the United States over all the channels of radio transmission; and to provide for the use of such channels, but not the ownership thereof, by persons for limited periods of time, under licenses granted by Federal authority, and no such license shall be construed to create any right, beyond the terms, conditions, and periods of the license. (47 USC Sec. 301)

With one-third of those 8,000 stations needing a renewal decision every year the Commission has evolved a system for processing the flow of paperwork.

All licenses in a given state expire on the same day, with states grouped to provide a rough equality of numbers of stations on each of the six renewal days each year.

For seven years I dissented every two months, both to the renewals and to the Commission's renewal process. Why? Because the FCC never seemed to *do* anything except renew every licensee's license. There were no criteria for evaluating licensees' performance. During the years I served I cannot recall a single instance in which the FCC set a station's renewal application for hearing on its own motion (that is, without public intervenors) for reasons of inadequate programming alone. Something less than one tenth of one percent were set for hearing for any reason – antitrust violations, fraud, discriminatory employment practices, or blatant, repeated refusal to comply with the fairness doctrine.

> *For seven years I dissented every two months, both to the renewals and to the Commission's renewal process. Why? Because the FCC never [did] anything except renew every licensee's license.*

Most of these dissenting opinions were necessarily brief and routine. It seemed futile to repeat the same arguments six times a year. Four ultimately became book-length studies, often with the assistance of Commissioner Ken Cox.

Of all my colleagues, Ken was probably the greatest influence on me during the first few months. A bright lawyer and law professor, he had come from Washington State to Washington, D.C., where he worked as special counsel for Washington's Senator Warren Magnuson. Senator Magnuson served on the

Senate Commerce Committee and introduced Ken to broadcast regulation from the Senate's perspective. He was appointed Chief of the Broadcast Bureau during FCC Chairman Newton Minow's term (1961-1963), took an active role in that position, and was appointed to a term as commissioner (1963-1970).

As Commissioner Ken Cox, he probably worked harder than any of the other commissioners. He was constantly taking notes in meetings. He was the only one I ever suspected read all the opinions. He would kindly explain them to his colleagues and arrive at meetings with the list of typographical errors discovered during the wee hours of the night before.

His experience as Broadcast Bureau Chief enabled him to retain the call letters and owners' names for a remarkably large number of stations. Most reassuring was the restoration he provided for my sanity.

It is emotionally, psychologically and intellectually difficult to perceive things 180 degrees out of phase from one's colleagues on a regular basis. It creates an Alice in Wonderland sensation to life inside the Commission. For starters, the characters in the subgovernment are often amusing in appearance, manner and speech. They can become comic caricatures of themselves. What they say so often makes absolutely no sense at all. When you point out what seem to be rather obvious logical inconsistencies or impending national disasters, the words do not seem to enter their consciousness. They just light up another cigar. In the midst of this environment it was warmly satisfying to find someone to talk to who not only understood what I was saying but seemed to agree with much of it.

Ken probably saw me as a potential additional vote for more meaningful programming regulation. He was right. To take action as a commissioner one must be able to count up to four – that is, it takes four commissioners to constitute a majority of seven. The challenge becomes one of picking up votes. Ken and I succeeded in counting up to two on a number of occasions, but we rarely managed three or four. The first book-length dissent we did to license renewals was our Oklahoma case study, 14 F.C.C. 2d 1-126 (1968).

My frustration with the Commission's failure to participate in the license renewal process in any meaningful way grew during the early months. I didn't want to criticize my colleagues unfairly, and Chairman Rosel Hyde promised that something would be done. But nothing ever was and eventually I grew tired of waiting. And so it was that, in January of 1967, Ken Cox and I began our partnership – although on this occasion we each wrote our own opinion. Mine follows.

Programming Responsibility – Renewal of Licenses for Stations in Florida, Puerto Rico, and the Virgin Islands
7 F.C.C. 2d, 122, 130 (1967)
Dissenting Opinion of Commissioner Nicholas Johnson

I dissent from the almost complete lack of concern for the programming performance and proposals of licensed stations the Commission evidences by this action.

It is appropriate that this Commission give attention to the painting and location of antenna towers, and that it enforces licensees' compliance with the engineering standards of frequency and power essential to an orderly national system of broadcasting. But to assume that such actions are the beginning and end of our responsibility in licensing radio stations seems, to me, to ignore what the broadcasting business and our statutory mandate are all about.

> *It is appropriate that [the FCC] give attention to the painting and location of antenna towers [but broadcasting] is programming ... probably the most powerful means of mass communications the human species ever turned loose upon itself. It gains its power not from kilowatts but from content, from its capacity to create and contort the mind and spirit of a nation.*

Broadcasting is programming. It is probably the most powerful means of mass communications the human species ever turned loose upon itself. It gains its power not from kilowatts but from content, from its capacity to create and contort the mind and spirit of a nation.

Individual broadcasters operate and program at the pleasure of the American people, as limited licensees of the public's airwaves. Most broadcasters of my acquaintance take this responsibility seriously – as conscientious citizens and as proud professional men and women, as well as in their capacity as responsible FCC licensees.

But this agency also has its responsibility: To renew the broadcasting licenses of none but those licensees serving the public interest. How can that responsibility best be exercised with regard to the programming product of the station owner?

I would be among the last to make hasty proposals as to how the Commission's responsibility can best be exercised. I would be among the first to caution of the real dangers of governmental abridgment of our freedoms of speech and press. Even had I the power to do so, I would be disinclined to impose my personal standards of taste upon millions of American listeners and viewers. Governmental previewing of all commercial radio and television shows, or the prescribing of their program formats, is, quite wisely, out of the question under our American system.

There are many paths open to a Commission in search of a responsible and effective way to contribute to better programming in the public interest. The alternatives need not be politically unrealistic, offensive to the broadcasting establishment, or appear the hallmark of a tough regulator. Indeed, some proposals might even be seen by the industry as far preferable to what they must now endure. I will suggest (without endorsement) some illustrative possibilities a little later in this opinion.

It is even conceivable that rational analysis might lead a reasonable man to conclude that the public interest in programming would be best served by encouraging broadcasters to select those program formats that will create the greatest possible advertising revenue. If that position – held by some broadcasters – has now been endorsed by the present Commission majority, as it appears to have been, I would prefer that we make this an explicit, public, reasoned judgment rather than go through the motions of appearing to review programming against a public-interest standard when in fact doing nothing of the sort.

> *[T]he Commission can do nothing until it is willing to alter its present complacent and comfortable hear-no-evil, see-no-evil slouch in front of the radio and television sets of America.*

But the Commission can do nothing until it is willing to alter its present complacent and comfortable hear-no-evil, see-no-evil slouch in front of the radio and television sets of America.

The matter presently before the Commission would appear to be relatively routine – if the staff and majority's response is any indication. In fact, that is the heart of the problem. The FCC's Broadcast Bureau is about to issue renewal licenses to 206 standard broadcast stations in Florida, Puerto Rico, and the Virgin Islands for three-year terms beginning February 1, 1967. Whether the authority to issue the renewals has been delegated by the Commission to the Bureau is unclear. In any event, the Bureau feels compelled to report its actions to the full

Commission and await word that its report has been noted before issuing the licenses. The Commission has duly noted the report and the licenses will issue.

The Commission's current ambivalence, born of the conflict between authority and inaction, is revealed in the searching questionnaire which each renewal applicant must fill out, but which is then put to little if any useful purpose whatsoever by the Commission. Each applicant for renewal must indicate what proportion of programming he or she proposes for a number of categories, such as news, public affairs, and "other" (meaning agricultural, religious, and instructional). Those applicants whose proposals the staff thinks might concern individual Commissioners are singled out for attention in the Bureau's report.

Let us examine them for a moment. Because Commissoner Cox has provided in his opinion a very thorough and useful analysis of these applicants' programming a summary will be adequate for my present purposes.

In the group whose applications for renewal the Commission now approves:

- Two stations propose no news programming whatsoever.
- Seven propose no public affairs programming – a total of 23 conceding they plan less than 1 percent.
- A total of 88 stations plan to spend less than 5 percent of their time on all "other" (agricultural, religious, and instructional) programming combined.

And note that these are "just promises." Promises that licensees can assume will be ignored by this Federal regulatory commission (judging by today's action). For the report also shows that although only 23 stations (over 10 percent of the group of 206) presently intend to program less than 1 percent "public affairs" during 1967, for the year 1966 not 23, but 49 of the 206 fell below this standard.

What is the point of pretending this is anything other than the total abdication of Commission responsibility that must be obvious to any casual observer? The point, of course, is that millions of Americans are reassured in the belief that there is an FCC in Washington, reassured in the assumption that the Federal Government is insisting the public's airwaves be operated in the public interest. The point is that, through inaction, the Government enables the occasional irresponsible broadcaster to walk the streets of his or her community with head high. Each licensee can be self-confident in the satisfaction that on her studio wall hang, side by side, two framed imprimaturs: the Seal of Good Practice from her industry association, and the FCC broadcasting license from her federal government. The existence of the FCC, like other governmental agencies, creates a sense of security and complacency for the citizenry, snug in its assumption that there is effective regulation. So assuming, it does not demand more.

Ultimately, of course, responsible regulators must formulate useful and appropriate procedures for Commission evaluation of programming in the public interest. In devising such procedures one would hope for means that are effective, appropriate, legal, fully considerate of the owner's investment and professional experience, and fully representative of local interests. But so long as we do that, the method we choose is in no sense as important as that we stop abiding the foolishness that section 326 ("nothing ... shall give the Commission the power of censorship ....") renders us impotent.

I agree with Commissioner Cox that – given the Commission's present standards and procedures and the past promises of these 206 licensees – the licenses of some of the broadcasters presently before us ought not to be renewed without further examination. I am much less certain, however, that the prescription of programming categories is necessarily the best long-range, overall approach for this Commission to take. Local conditions do vary. This variance, this diversity, is at the heart of the greatness of America – and its broadcasting system. It may be as foolish for a New York City station to carry farm news as it would be irresponsible for a rural Iowa station not to.

Moreover, the number of stations in a community are relevant in evaluating the programming of each. Presumably, most people would agree that broadcasters in one- or two-station markets should program a wide variety of services – including a substantial amount of news and public affairs. In the major markets, where 10 or 20 stations may be available, the listener may be able to receive an all-news station, the networks' news and other programming, and a community or educational station providing treatment of local issues. Considering the programming available to such a community as a whole, it may be that little harm is done by other stations providing mostly talk shows, classical music, or rock-and-roll. But these are not the extremes we deal with today.

Perhaps, rather than devising a more effective role for the FCC, we (and the broadcasting industry) should welcome greater public participation in program judgments. Would some well-publicized, community-wide local hearings into the public service of selected radio stations – like those in Chicago and Omaha for television stations – be useful at the time of license renewals? Should we provide more meaningful opportunity for applicants competing for those stations doing least well in serving their communities? Should we make efforts to encourage more letter-writing from the public to the FCC and the broadcasters? Could ratings services, or other polling techniques, be turned to better advantage? Should we provide more precise procedures to be used by broadcasters in surveying the programming needs of the communities they serve? Would it be useful for someone, perhaps the broadcasters themselves, to identify the most important issues confronting the communities involved and the broadcasters' response to those issues? Could periodic, publicized, transcribed, open-mike programs, inviting public comment on the station's service, be turned to useful purpose? In polling public opinion, how can we gather information about possible listener and viewer preference for the kinds of alternative programming they are not now receiving and have not experienced?

Another area of potential Commission activity with significant impact on programming diversity, if not quality, are regulations of the often anticompetitive and restrictive practices surrounding program creation, procurement, and distribution by networks and others.

The creation and support of noncommercial, experimental, educational public television represents another area of potential Commission activity affecting the quality and variety of programming fare received by America's listeners and viewers.

Such observations are certainly not exhaustive or dispositive, and some may not even be relevant. But even this brief survey is sufficient to suggest the magnitude and depth of issues and alternatives that must be explored.

Certainly I am very mindful of the complexity and sensitivity of the issues involved. Many wise, experienced, and responsible men and women have struggled with them in the past; undoubtedly many more will do so in the years to come. Any judgments or even concerns which I express now are, of course, tentative. But the problems are so central to the FCC's effective and meaningful functioning that I believe it useful for commissioners to state their positions from time to time – whatever they may be. My predecessors and colleagues followed this practice, and I have chosen this occasion to do so. Obviously, the issues warrant far more from a commissioner than the cursory initial comments I have set forth in this opinion. Hopefully, in the months and years to come I may be able at least to participate in the kind of more substantial contribution I have called for.

Two conclusions are clear. First, there are many courses open to us that could vastly improve broadcasting and its vital role in our society without engaging in the fruitless debate about possible censorship that leaves us divided and motionless. Second, within the experience of this Commission, America's great broadcasting industry, and its thoughtful students and critics, simply must lie viable alternatives to the abdication of responsibility evidenced by the Commission's approach to the renewals approved today.

This was to be one of the most naïve, open and conciliatory opinions I would ever write about programming regulation. Notwithstanding my colleagues' participation in the ABC-ITT case I was still giving them the benefit of the doubt. Perhaps there were some reasons for using one approach to programming regulation rather than another. Perhaps they would be interested in considering the alternatives. With the passage of the months it became clear they were interested in neither reasons nor alternatives. To continue doing nothing, as they were, was indefensible. Nonetheless to consider the matter at all would open a Pandora's box they preferred be left closed.

Having said that, the opinion looks good almost a decade later. The suggestions regarding greater public participation in the process were taken up by the public and courts, though not the FCC. Community hearings were tried by the FCC in 1974. Competing applicants were forthcoming. The Commission later experimented with both the notion of community surveys, called ascertainment, and programming responsive to identified community issues. Correspondence from the public is now kept in public files. The FCC requires stations to make announcements inviting public comments. Open mike programs flourished. Anticompetitive program production practices were targeted by the Department of Justice in a suit against the networks, and the FCC with its primetime access rule. Although the FCC never gave public broadcasting the support it should have, the Corporation for Public Broadcasting was established.

Considering that it was all contained in one paragraph, as a brief survey of some issues and alternatives, by a freshman commissioner in January 1967, it has held up well.

But the Commission has still not established programming standards for license renewals. Commissioner Cox and I remained hopeful it might. So we continued to grind out our bi-monthly dissents and occasional book-length reports.

We began, as the Florida opinion indicates by simply singling out for notation and comment those broadcasters proposing to devote less than five percent of their programming time to news, less than one percent to public affairs, or less than five percent to all other programming exclusive of entertainment and sports – what came to be called the 5-1-5 standard.

This never impressed our colleagues, but we were informed that some stations' lawyers were advising their clients to meet the 5-1-5 levels just to avoid the dissenting opinion. After all, we weren't asking for much. Five percent of an hour is three minutes. Five percent of programming as news would mean a 15-minute newscast every five hours, or one minute thirty seconds on the hour and half-hour, or some other combination.

In 1968 we undertook our first book-length inquiry. *Broadcasting in America and the FCC's License Renewal Process: An Oklahoma Case Study*, 14 F.C.C. 2d 1-126 (1968). We selected it partly because the Oklahoma renewals were next in line, but also because the state was typical. Our mail and the academic literature provided no reason to believe it was better or worse than others. The state is nineteenth in size, was then 27th in population, and contained both the country's 37th largest television market (Oklahoma City) and some of the most sparsely populated territory in the nation. Its population centers receive radio and television signals from in-state stations, unlike New Jersey and some other states.

> **As far as Oklahoma broadcasting is concerned, the concept of local service is largely a myth.**

We did an analysis of ownership patterns (concentrated), print and broadcast media in 12 representative cities (limited), and programming performance of the stations (mediocre) with emphasis on *local* programming (very little).

Our conclusion was "As far as Oklahoma broadcasting is concerned, the concept of local service is largely a myth." There were 10 commercial television stations; they grossed $16 million a year. Three had less than eight hours of news of any kind during the week. No station had a regularly scheduled primetime program devoted to controversial issues in the state or community. No station carried as much as one hour of locally originated programming in primetime except for news. We pleaded with our colleagues to establish *some* system for reviewing the programming performance of stations at license renewal time. They were unmoved. All of the Oklahoma stations were renewed.

Our approach to the Oklahoma renewals having failed, in 1969 we turned to comparative statistical analyses for the renewals in New York (18 F.C.C. 2d 269) and Washington, D.C. (21 F.C.C. 2d 35).

For the stations in our New York Report there were 21 tables of comparative statistical analysis. Always using the stations' own information, we ranked them by proportion of their programming that was news, public affairs, or other-than-entertainment; the extent of their failure to carry network news and public affairs programming (a number of ABC affiliates didn't carry their network's evening news); local programming in primetime; local and regional news as a proportion of all news; proportion of employees handling news; number of commercials; number of public service announcements; and each station's financial resources.

We prepared a comparative ranking of the 24 New York stations. Once again our colleagues were unresponsive; 24 license renewal requests were submitted and 24 licenses were renewed. It is unlikely more than one or two commissioners, if any, read more than a couple pages of our Report.

But then a funny thing began to happen. We got an irate letter from one of the station's lawyers. His client had been ranked somewhere in the twenties, and the lawyer's elaborate computation proved, he contended, that we had ranked his client a couple of places too low. We were ecstatic. If anyone cared whether they were ranked 21 or 23 on our list we were getting through.

It appeared that rankings and disclosure could be a form of regulation for minority commissioners and members of the public otherwise excluded from the process. Rankings done regularly and publicly are of great concern to those being evaluated. They have the potential to improve the performance of the worst and encourage the best. Some stations used their favorable rankings in promotional materials. Not insignificantly, journalists may view such data and information as news.

Finally, by using the broadcasters' own data two things were accomplished. First, there would be few complaints the raw data was inaccurate, skewed to reflect adversely on the industry, or reflected our subjective evaluations. Second, no broadcasting company could complain that it was being held to impossibly high standards when those standards merely reflected the performance of their similarly-situated competitors.

If there are benefits to regulation with irrefutable numbers and the elimination of subjective judgments, so are there limitations. Counting minutes of news eliminates distinctions between news limited to auto accidents, fires, holdups, weather and sports and news from stations devoting money and time to investigative reporting. Public service announcements dealing with controversial subjects such as sending checks to the American Cancer Society, joining the Army, or not standing up in canoes, count just as heavily as spots prepared by community activists dealing with unjustifiably high utility rates, a local factory's pollution, or favoritism of the rich in assessing property taxes.

We believed subjective evaluations of content should be left to local residents or academic researchers on the scene. It would be inappropriate for FCC commissioners to go beyond the hard data we had. Later in 1969 when we undertook a study of renewals in D.C., Maryland, Virginia and West Virginia, a local group had done its own study, modeled on our New York Report, and we simply reprinted it (21 F.C.C. 2d 35-140).

The culmination of this approach came after Ken Cox had left the Commission. His term expired in 1970. (Although Ken was interested in his job, brilliant, fair, respected by broadcasters, Congress and the academic community alike, and wanted to continue serving, President Nixon refused to reappoint him.)

We increased the number of young people with access to an FCC commissioner's office by my offering a seminar in communications policy through the Georgetown University Law School (for no pay). The meetings were held in the FCC offices in the evenings and dealt with FCC cases. In 1973 one such group worked with our office to produce a book-length analysis of television stations in the 50 largest cities. (*Broadcasting in America*, 42 F.C.C. 2d 1-172 (1973).

That was our last effort to get the FCC commissioners interested in the programming performance of their licensees. Cox was already gone, and I was soon to leave. Under the leadership of academician-facilitator-consultant Dr. Barry Cole the FCC does now gather and publish much of the information we were trying to present in the *Broadcasting in America* report. But I am still unaware, as of this writing, of any licenses being set for renewal hearings because of the failure of a broadcasting station to fulfill its programming obligations to its local community.

Of course, the bi-monthly license renewal process is only the most regular and systematic of the Commission's evaluation of its licensees' performance. The Commission is also confronted with other complaints and revelations about broadcasters that must be disposed of in some way – as the next chapter illustrates.

178 – Catfish Solution

Chapter Nine
The Short Arm of the Law: Six FCC Efforts at Enforcement

As the following excerpts from six opinions reveal, the agency's intellectual ingenuity reaches a fever pitch when confronted with the challenge of keeping licensees in the profitable business called broadcasting notwithstanding their clear violations of Commission standards. You will soon see how the FCC can find 33 minutes of commercials per hour, a proposal for no news programming whatsoever, racist programming, and out-and-out fraud all consistent with "the public interest." You will see how fast the Broadcast Bureau can work when necessary to avoid a citizens' license challenge, and how NBC can get off scot-free with eight serious charges raised against it.

Application of Accomack-Northampton
Broadcasting Co.
8 F.C.C. 2d 357 (1967)
Dissenting Statement of Commissioner Nicholas
Johnson

The standard generally accepted for [stations' percentage of commercial content] — by the Commission's general questionnaire and the National Association of Broadcasters Code of Good Practices — is a maximum of 18 minutes of commercials per hour (roughly one out of every three minutes). Although this applicant appears at first blush to comply with the 18-

minute standard, a careful reading of its conditions and exceptions indicates its standard will be, in fact, "not normally expected to exceed" 33 minutes of commercials per hour.

Here is how the applicant expresses its standard: The maximum amount of commercial matter in any 60-minute segment which the applicant normally proposes is 18 minutes. The applicant further states that in order to fulfill its obligations to the public and maintain its economic health, the proposed station will find it necessary to increase the percentage of commercial time during special occasions such as before elections, Christmas, Old Timers Days, Thanksgiving, during vegetable harvest time, and during periods immediately after an outage due to equipment failures; however, during these periods the commercial time is not normally expected to exceed about 55 percent in any hour. It is not normally expected to occur on more than about two or three days in any typical composite week.

> *When the broadcasting industry and Congress were first considering Federal regulation of broadcasting it was Secretary of Commerce Herbert C. Hoover who said, "It is inconceivable that we should allow so great a possibility for service to be drowned in advertising chatter."*

I feel constrained to make the observation that, while the issues posed by this case are deep and broad, under our present procedures the outcome in the individual case is really of relatively little significance.

Some would agree with this observation and conclude that, therefore, the Commission should not regulate advertising content at all, leaving the matter wholly in the hands of the station operator. The "public interest" served by such a role is presumably a listener's option to turn either his or her station selector knob or on-off switch. The administrative ease offered by such a course is appealing. The administrative responsibility I find less attractive.

In any event, such cases now come before us; they must be responsibly disposed of.

Few issues in the history of broadcasting have created as much concern and as little consensus as what to do about advertising.

- In the 1920's industry and Government representatives alike expressed concern lest this new information medium of radio be turned to private profit at public expense. Congress gave the matter its attention.
- Today the industry recognizes in its Code of Good Practices that commercial practices are relevant to broadcasting in the public interest.
- Congress – even those members concerned about Commission rulemaking regarding commercial practices – recognizes the propriety and desirability of some form of Commission regulation of advertising.
- The Commission has, since its earliest days, regulated advertising policies – and been consistently encouraged and supported by the

courts in doing so.

- Finally, even if one adopts the slogan that "the public interest is what interests the public," the Commission's mail would seem to confirm that little interests the listening public more than commercial practices.

The principal question, therefore, is not whether, but what to do about advertising in broadcasting – and who should do it. Even a Commission decision to do nothing (or to delegate to the industry), if that be its view, ought to be adequately analyzed and explained as a form of Commission action in terms of the public interest. Many relevant questions are, however, for me, as yet unanswered. I believe they should be addressed in something other than a case-by-case environment. What is the FCC doing? Why? At what price? To produce what result? What alternative paths are there to the same goal? Why is our present way the best?

Recently I characterized the Commission's fulfillment of its responsibility to uphold the public interest in the quantity of broadcast advertising in these words:

> *Regulation of commercial content by the FCC has always been a concern to you (the broadcasting industry). It requires a substantial effort by the Commission staff. And yet, the FCC has not only failed to enforce standards any stricter than your own, it has actually tended to depress the broadcasting industry's code standards to lower levels. It was only by dint of industry pressure that the FCC raised its standards from 20 to 18 minutes of commercials per radio hour to comply*

with your code. Now the FCC is eroding standards once more by waiver and exception, and I gather the code may give up the fight in despair. Given this FCC record the public interest might be better served if the industry were left to regulate itself. If that be the case, and there be no hope for reforming the agency, even basic principles of cost-conscious management would dictate the FCC invest its staff's time elsewhere.

"Reevaluating the Regulatory Role," speech to the Iowa Association of Broadcasters, May 13, 1967.

It was recently reported in *Broadcasting* magazine:

In effect, he [Howard Bell, NAB code director] complained that the Commission had forced the NAB to make its 18-minute rule more flexible. "We were in the posture of being rigid and inflexible" on the time limits allowed, "and the FCC was more permissive," he said.

At the time I had no idea the characterization would so soon be borne out. Here is a perfect example. It is disgusting and discouraging, hilarious and serious, but seems to be firmly fixed as Commission policy. ...

When the broadcasting industry and Congress were first considering Federal regulation of broadcasting it was Secretary of Commerce Herbert C. Hoover who said, "It is inconceivable that we should allow so great a possibility for service to be drowned in advertising chatter." Who in the 1934 Congress would have predicted that its emphasis on "the public interest" in the then new Communications Act would be used to sanction 33 minutes of commercials per broadcast hour a mere 33 years later? Can the public be offered nothing save the realization that, at this rate, by 1994 the radio hour will be totally consumed with commercials?

Application of Herman C. Hall
11 F.C.C. 2d 344 (1968)
Dissenting Opinion of
Commissioners Kenneth A. Cox and Nicholas Johnson

"No news is good news" has today become the motto of the FCC for the 120,000 citizens of Greensboro, N.C. For no news is precisely what Greensboro citizens tuning into WMDE-FM are going to be hearing in the near future as a result of today's decision. ...

> **The staff noted the assignee's disarmingly frank promise to broadcast literally no news or public affairs.**

The staff conceded that Hilker was acquiring his 10th broadcast interest, and that all are in a very limited region of the country. Yet such an array of communications media produces no problems of concentration, it was urged, because most of the outlets are located in small cities with populations under 18,000. Why we should suddenly be less concerned about would-be communications monopolists in small towns than in large cities was not made clear. Roughly 70 million of 200 million Americans live on farms and in towns under 20,000 population. That is certainly true for many of North Carolina's 4.9 million residents. Presumably, they have just as much right as New Yorkers to more than one window on the world outside (and inside) their communities. I earlier addressed this issue in a case involving the 7,794 residents of Paris, Ky.

The staff also noted the assignee's disarmingly frank promise to broadcast literally no news or public affairs programs whatsoever. This proposed programming, the Commission was told, should be no cause for alarm – and certainly no cause for holding a hearing. Hilker had surveyed eight citizens, the staff explained, on the basis of which he determined that Greensboro did not need any additional outlets for news and public affairs beyond the other radio and television stations and newspapers operating in the city.

In terms of numbers of people affected, this case is not an important one. But to the people in typical communities in North Carolina within the listening range of Hilker's 10 stations, its consequences are both crucial and very unfortunate indeed.

Lamar Life Broadcasting Co. (WLBT)
14 F.C.C. 2d 431, 442, 463-467 (1968)
Dissenting Opinion of
Commissioners Kenneth A. Cox and Nicholas Johnson

Part V. United Church of Christ versus the Federal Communications Commission: A Landmark on the Road to Where?

In recent months and years the Federal Communications Commission has been the target of continuing and sharply critical comment from Congress, the courts, the executive branch, the press, the academic and research community, and even from its own members – one of whom (neither of us) recently recommended the abolition of the agency. While some of this criticism is unfair, this state of affairs is largely of the Commission's own making. We believe that this case will, with reason, give rise to renewed attacks upon the agency.

Were it not so serious, and an actual case affecting the rights of the parties and the public in the Jackson area, this culmination of the church's efforts in a license renewal proceeding could be considered a classic caricature of the FCC at its worst. But for the majority's opinion here, no one would be likely to imagine the Commission capable of reaching so unsound a result or showing so transparent a disregard of the practices reflected on this record, or that it would do so at this of all times in American history, or at the expense of these complainants.

For this case has everything. A racist television station in Mississippi. An offended citizenry that actually takes the expensive and frustrating course of involving itself in the license renewal process. A church as a party. Negroes protesting the programming abuse received by that nearly 50 percent of the people in the station's viewing area who are black. A landmark, first-impression decision by the U.S. court of appeals awarding "standing" to such parties. The station's misrepresentations to the Commission over the years. The Commission's contortions to keep the public out entirely, then to place upon them an impossible burden of proof, then to reverse long-held precedents and ignore the clear suggestions of the court as to the standards to be applied. This disappointing saga has now ended with a finding by this Commission that the station has been serving "the public interest" and is entitled to a regular, three-year license renewal. Note what the majority has succeeded in doing by this single action.

The record reveals that the United Church of Christ and its allies apparently have been regarded within the Commission as a kind of unfamiliar pestilence, to be scourged through harassment, the piling up of procedural obstructions, and the denial of rights clearly granted them by a reviewing court in this very same case.

The Commission has gritted its teeth and set its face against public participation in agency proceedings at a moment when "participatory democracy" rides the crest of a wave of mass enthusiasm which has already become a major national movement. Everyone, from States' Righters to New Leftists, from the upper echelons of the establishment to the storefronts of the ghetto, has embraced the ideal of extending democracy in all levels of government – everyone, that is, except for this FCC majority.

The Commission has been criticized for treating the absence of public complaints as evidence of service to "the public interest," minimizing the FCC's responsibility to make an independent investigation. The Commission today shows its strong distaste for the presence of a complaint, even though (or perhaps because it was) pressed with dedication and persistence by those representing nearly 50 percent of the population in a community served by the licensee. The record reveals that the United Church of Christ and its allies apparently have been regarded within the Commission as a kind of unfamiliar pestilence, to be scourged through harassment, the piling up of procedural obstructions, and the denial of rights clearly granted them by a reviewing court in this very same case.

Great public concern has been focused on the role of broadcasting in fostering communication between the races. The Kerner Commission devoted an entire chapter of its *Report of the National Advisory Commission on Civil Disorders* (Kerner Commission, 1968) to the news media and their potential contribution to improved race relations. The FCC's Chairman Hyde has termed this "not just another story – another 'issue of public importance' ... [but] a crisis ...." We have recently witnessed the assassinations of Dr. Martin Luther King and Senator Robert F. Kennedy, the outbreak of violence in our Nation's capital, and the Poor Peoples March on Washington. A new presidential commission has just been established to study, among other things, the possible relation between television programming and violence. And yet the FCC majority picks this moment to find "the public interest" served by the renewal of a license for a station which has not only made no effort to include and serve Negroes, but which has for a decade maintained blatantly racist programming policies.

Public concern is rising about the growing tendency of protest movements to take to the streets, and even the techniques of civil disobedience, to compensate for their inability to find expression for their views on the mass media. How does this Commission respond? It responds by leaving the doctrine of broadcast fairness lifeless on the shelf. It responds by blithely renewing the license of an owner who systematically used one of two television stations in the capital of Mississippi to suppress the expression of views favorable to integration.

The obligation of local broadcast stations to provide local service has recently been reaffirmed and defended by members of the FCC as well as by representatives of the broadcasting industry who are concerned about the new technologies that might replace the present system of local broadcasting with nationwide wire or satellite-based systems. And yet the FCC has today refused to discipline a licensee which pursued a policy of deliberate and positive disservice to one-half of its viewing public.

What, one might ask, does the Commission majority expect representative public groups to do in their participation in license renewal proceedings? The court of appeals has said that "responsible and representative groups eligible to intervene ...; such community organizations as civic associations, professional societies, unions, churches, and educational institutions or associations might well be helpful to the Commission." The court is right. Well, here is a group that tried – and failed – in what one would think was a rather extreme case. The court says that "some mechanism must be developed so that the legitimate interests of listeners can be made a part of the record which the Commission evaluates." What is that mechanism to be if this was not enough?

Much of the problem, we believe, derives from the FCC majority's mischaracterization of the nature of the broadcaster's responsibility and the public's rights in the license renewal process. As the court said, "After nearly five decades of operation the broadcasting industry does not seem to have grasped the simple fact that a broadcast license is a public trust subject to termination for breach of duty." What is that duty? To serve "the needs, tastes, and interests" of the listeners and viewers of that station. Responsible broadcasters not only tolerate, but actively seek out, the views of local citizens. It is good business as well as responsible licensee conduct.

For the broadcaster is, in effect, an elected public official, using the property of his or her audience (the public's airwaves) to make private profit. He or she holds a three-year trust – not a property right – to operate a local station. The burden is upon him or her to demonstrate, at every three-year license renewal, that he or she has been a faithful trustee. The burden is not upon the protesting public to prove that a broadcaster's "rights" should be denied. Frivolous or malicious complaints, or those inspired by economic competitors, must, of course, be weighed appropriately. But when "responsible and representative groups" have opinions, grievances and "legitimate interests" we think they should be received hospitably and given serious weight by this Commission.

It should be noted that the citizen participants in this case were able to employ a resource which is unavailable to most members of the viewing public. The United Church of Christ was able to hire a lawyer. But it should be possible for a citizen to participate in a license renewal proceeding without a lawyer. Careful monitoring studies are desirable; they are an effective form of advocacy. But a citizen who complains of a given station, and provides the date and time of the program and a general description of the offending matter, should be able to rest upon that evidence, leaving the station with the burden of refuting the charge or explaining the programming. If the time should come when we believe the Commission's procedures are being abused, or its licensees are being harassed, there are remedies enough that can then be applied. We are talking about otherwise busily occupied American citizens – like most of us – who have no familiarity with procedural niceties, but who may try to make their voices heard on one of the most significant issues in communities across this country: Radio and television programming. And participating in FCC proceedings should be, for them, as easy as attending a PTA meeting, a zoning board hearing, or voting in a city council election. They should be welcomed by this Commission, not put off or held to unreasonable requirements.

The Commission majority has often seemed loathe to express any views with regard to the programming performance of licensees. The ostensible rationale, to the extent one exists, is that programming matters are best worked out in the local community, between the broadcaster and the audience. We are sympathetic to this point of view. Given the choice, we would far prefer meaningful local participation in programming choices to decisions by seven FCC Commissioners in Washington. But we emphasize the word "meaningful." The public must really know of its rights – not just be able to find out about them in the United States Code, the Code of Federal Regulations, and the legal notices (and equivalent radio and television announcements) in the local community. It must know how to exercise those rights: The difference between a casual letter to a station or the FCC, and a petition for intervention in a license renewal proceeding. It must know its options in programming – not just be asked whether it likes a given station or not, or whether it has any new ideas. Participation in programming choices and FCC proceedings must be encouraged – not frustrated at every turn. The court has observed that –

> *Public participation is especially important in a renewal proceeding, since the public will have been exposed for at least three years to the licensee's performance ... [and] may be the only objectors. ... [Consumers] are generally among the best vindicators of the public interest. In order to safeguard the public interest in broadcasting, therefore, we hold that some "audience participation" must be allowed in license renewal proceedings.*

We agree. The majority professes to – in those cases in which no representatives of the public appear, and their absence is read as public endorsement. But abdication of the responsibility of the Federal Communications Commission to the citizens of local communities is only justifiable if there is someone there to assume it. Abdication coupled with positive efforts to prevent public participation boarders on protection of broadcasters' interests at any cost. And, indeed, even the interests of the protected industry are little served by leaving the occasional irresponsible broadcaster free to flaunt the public interest and soil the reputation of colleagues.

> *[I]t would appear that the only way in which members of the public can prevent renewal of an unworthy station's license is to steal the document from the wall of the station's studio in the dead of night or hope that the courts will do more than merely review and remand cases to the FCC with instructions that may be ignored.*

We are saddened that our colleagues, as well as some members of the Commission's staff, seem so indifferent to the agency's responsibilities and to the needs of the times. But, more than that, we are disturbed at the majority's willingness to go to such great lengths to protect a licensee with a very bad record. It has ignored what we believe the court of appeals directed us to do. It has rejected or overlooked what we regard as valid evidence – all to avoid reaching unwanted results. It has sanctioned obstruction and procedural harassment which can only discourage and defeat citizen intruders so bold as to venture to exercise rights guaranteed them by law. Indeed, it would appear that the only way in which members of the public can prevent renewal of an unworthy station's license is to steal the document from the wall of the station's studio in the dead of night or hope that the courts will do more than merely review and remand cases to the FCC with instructions that may be ignored.

Application of Star Stations of Indiana, Inc. (WIFE AM-FM)
19 F.C.C. 2d 991, 996 (1969)
Dissenting Opinion of Commissioner Nicholas Johnson in which Commissioner Kenneth A. Cox Joins

The result reached here is truly shocking. In an astonishing opinion, the majority has concluded that, although the licensee of WIFE (AM) in Indianapolis, Ind., fraudulently deceived its clients with respect to certain promotional contests and bilked its advertisers of more than $6,000 in advertising revenues (all during a one-year probationary license renewal period), the licensee's operation has nevertheless "minimally met the public interest standard" and its license should be renewed.

If fraud and deception of more than $6,000 are minimally in accordance with the public interest, then I think it must be apparent to all that the FCC's attempts at serving the public interest are themselves without even minimal standards. ...

Briefly, on October 28, 1964, this Commission found that the licensee of WIFE and WIFE-FM had "hypoed" its ratings by using an audience rating report made during a period when the station was conducting an intensive give-away contest. The Commission found that the licensee's conduct fell "considerably short of the degree of responsibility in the operation of a broadcast station which the Commission has the right to expect of a licensee." ... Nevertheless, we decided to grant the licensee a probationary 1-year license renewal, from August 1, 1964, to August 1, 1965, "affording the Commission," as we said then, "an early opportunity to re-examine your operations and determine the degree of responsibility which you have exhibited during the year."

> *Has not the time come simply to say that when licensees, on repeated occasions, hypo ratings, conduct fraudulent contests, and defraud advertisers out of thousands of dollars, they have lost their right to function as a trustee for public property?*

On May 17, 1965, applications for renewal of the licenses of WIFE and WLFE-FM were filed. On September 14, 1965, the Commission received its first indication that WIFE had fraudulently falsified its bills to advertisers in a letter of complaint from the Central Indiana Better Business Bureau. ...

Today the Commission finally reaches that long-awaited re-examination of the licensee's qualifications which it promised in 1964. Despite blatant and admitted fraudulent misconduct by the licensee, despite the licensee's probationary one-year-renewal status, and despite the findings and recommendations of the hearing examiner to deny renewal of the WIFE-AM-FM licenses, the licensee is again let off merely with a warning – which I am forced to assume means as little now as it apparently did in 1964.

The majority does not attempt to dispute the licensee's misconduct in any respect. ... [T]he majority agrees with the examiner that WIFE's actions were fraudulent – that the licensee falsely told the sponsor of a contest that there had been winners when there were none, and then collected the prizes and gave them to station employees. Quite properly, the majority holds the licensee of WIFE-AM-FM "fully responsible for the conduct of its officers" even though the fraud may have been initially perpetrated by officers below the ownership level.

More importantly, the majority also finds that the licensee, on numerous occasions, furnished to clients "false and misleading information with respect to the times and dates purchased advertising was broadcast." Spot announcements, for example, were deliberately broadcast at times outside the time called for by the contracts (and upon occasion were not run at all) – apparently when time was not available within the specified time segments. In preparing the bills for the spot announcements, WIFE utilized a variety of means in order to keep advertisers from being alerted as to what was transpiring. One such method was the preparation of signed and executed affidavits which effectively served to lull unsuspecting advertisers into the mistaken belief that the commercials set forth were actually broadcast according to the official station log. In actual fact, the bills were not prepared from the logs at all.

The record also reveals that the customer was either billed off the orders, *i.e.*, on the basis of what she had ordered rather than on the basis of what the station log disclosed that she had received, or from an intermediate "recap" sheet on which entries abstracted from the logs were forced into the proper time segments. The net result was that a minimum of $6,101.43 was paid by advertisers for spot announcements which either had not been carried or which were run in time segments for which a lesser charge should have been assessed.

What is more, the licensee took no steps to ensure that blatant fraud such as this could not happen. Indeed, it deliberately abandoned a control book used by an earlier manager to prevent just such fraud – again as the majority acknowledges. Confronted by all this, the majority concludes: "It is undisputed that false bills were issued and that the ultimate responsibility for this practice lies with Burden," the station's principal owner.

Presented with clear, acknowledged, and repeated fraud by the licensee, during a probationary period which would normally call for higher than average performance, what does the majority conclude? Its conclusion, a cosmic non sequitur, can only be described as a pathetic equivocation: "*This is a very difficult and close case.*" [Emphasis added.] How many other Federal regulatory agencies, when shown clear and repeated cases of fraud, could still describe them as posing "a very difficult and close case"?

Despite this closeness, however, and without much apparent strain, the majority finds itself able quickly to conclude (a mere three sentences later) that WIFE has, after all, "minimally met the public interest standard," and that "denial of renewal is not required in the public interest. ..."

What public interest? If more than $6,000 worth of fraud is minimally consistent with the public interest, is there anything a licensee could do that would not meet this minimal public interest?

Their conclusion reached, the majority then falls comfortably back into the tired rhetoric of how the Commission (of course) will henceforth hold the licensee to very high standards of performance. Yet is it not perfectly clear from this decision that the Commission majority appears willing to whitewash almost any sort of licensee misconduct – including substantial involvement in dishonest practices?

Is it not ironic, for example, that the Commission majority is willing to admonish a television station for purportedly inducing criminal conduct (such as the smoking of marijuana, see Columbia Broadcasting System (WBBM-TV), 18 F.C.C. 2d 124, 142 (1969), yet excuse a licensee when that licensee itself commits what may very well be a crime? And is it not equally ironic that on the same day that the Commission finds repeated fraud by WIFE to be minimally in the public interest and renews the licenses of WIFE-AM-FM without imposing even a monetary fine, it levies numerous fines on other stations for far less culpable behavior – $700 on WKVA in Lewistown, Pa. (failure to make field intensity measurements and excessive modulation), $500 on WSNO in Barre, Bt. (operating above power), $2,000 on KFLN in Baker, Mont. (logging violations, excessive power, and post-sunset operation), $500 on KWMC in Del Rio, Tex., (unauthorized operator, logging violations), and $7,500 on WVOZ in Caroline, Puerto Rico (overmodulation, excessive power after sunset, and false logging)? Is there any doubt that this Commission too often reserves punitive action for smaller licensees? Is there any lingering doubt that the majority's marked disinclination to enforce its rules and policies by revocation of valuable broadcast properties simply enshrines the precept that the wealthier and more influential any broadcaster becomes, the more immune he or she is to regulation? Can there be any doubt left that there is something very wrong with the will of this agency to discharge its responsibilities to the public?

I cannot agree with the assertion that revocation of WIFE's license would "produce judgments in which lesser offenses require greater penalties, while the greater offense is less impugned." In actual fact, the majority has adopted an opinion in which "the greater offense" [*i.e.*, fraud] receives no penalty at all. The cases cited for the proposition that the Commission has "consistently ordered monetary forfeitures" and not license revocation "in every case of fraudulent billing" are inapposite. The offenses in those cases did not occur during a probationary one-year license renewal period, were generally far fewer in number than here, and involved far less money than WIFE's repeated fraud.

Nor can I agree with the statement that "[the] disparity of consequences between a monetary forfeiture and the denial of a license is so great that the severity of a denial, based on the inconclusive facts of this case, results in a refutation of the principles of administrative fairness." I fear that this position may have serious consequences for this Commission's attempts to regulate the broadcasting industry. If followed, it might rapidly become an apologia for deference to wealth, placing the larger and wealthier broadcasters beyond the reach of the Commission's regulations. If a majority of this Commission finds itself unable to grasp the nettle of license revocation – for the wealthier broadcaster as well as the smaller and less experienced – than I am afraid the Commission will lose its credibility as an even-handed regulatory agency in the eyes of the American public.

One can read and re-read the majority's opinion and find scant recital of any mitigating factors which might excuse the licensee for the fraud committed by WIFE. The only justification even attempted by the majority (and off-handedly at that) is the conclusory assertion that:

> [We] credit Burden [the licensee's controlling stockholder] with lack of knowledge and recognized that not only has some restitution been made, but that the licensee has voluntarily unearthed and made reimbursement in regard to additional infractions.

Utterly fantastic. If the latter part of this assertion is truly taken seriously, one can only assume the majority will tend to excuse fraud so long as the licensee makes restitution when caught and cooperates with the Commission in discovering additional wrong doing in which it has been involved and apprehended. ...

Although the record does not contain undisputed evidence that Burden had knowledge of the actual billing practices, it is difficult to conclude, in light of his apparent knowledge that spots were being moved from contracted period coupled with other evidence of record, that he was unaware of the fraud perpetrated on WIFE's advertisers. ...

Further, this position, if pushed to its logical conclusion, would place the burden of proving actual knowledge on the Commission – a burden which would grow in difficulty as the complexity of the licensee's managerial organization increased. Responsibility is already substantially diffused throughout the corporate hierarchies of many large licensees. And when this Commission is alerted to charges of "payola," or news "staging." or fraudulent billing, its investigations often run into a blank wall.

Thus, we may be told that the chair of the board was out of the country at the time, the president of the corporation wasn't told of these things, none of the numerous vice presidents were in charge of that particular problem, the general manager had issued instructions that the given offense was never to occur, his or her assistant didn't see it happen, and lower ranked employees were fired last week (for "unrelated reasons," of course) – but in any case, "it will never happen again." The problem is finding out "who's in charge here?"...

The majority today gives the licensee yet another chance to demonstrate that it can operate its station in the public interest, and repeats the same warning given it with the last one-year renewal. How many chances must we give licensees for fraud or other misconduct? Has not the time come simply to say that when licensees, on repeated occasions, hypo ratings, conduct fraudulent contests, and defraud advertisers out of thousands of dollars, they have lost their right to function as a trustee for public property?

One final point warrants special emphasis. The disposition of this case may determine for years to come the usefulness of the short-term renewal. The power to grant short-term renewals in doubtful situations can be extremely useful in obtaining operation in the public interest where a licensee's operation, while not entirely satisfactory, does not warrant absolute disqualification. However, if this is to be a meaningful compliance procedure, the licensee on a short-term renewal must be expected to improve the operation and to be diligent in maintaining proper standards. ...

If this Commission refuses to adopt programming standards, continues to grant engineering violation waivers, and persists in ignoring undue concentrations of media control, then the very least it can do is hold its licensees to accepted standards of business behavior. This agency should at least protect other businesses that must deal with broadcasters on a commercial basis. It is highly significant to note that the Commission first learned of WIFE's fraudulent billing practices, not from a member of the listening public, but from the Central Indiana Better Business Bureau, representing businesses in the Indianapolis area. Apparently a competitor of WIFE monitored the station's broadcasts (which is apparently more than WIFE's owner did) and then informed Amalie Oil, a WIFE advertiser, that its spots were not being carried at times specified in the contract and the affidavit-accompanied bills. I imagine the Central Indiana Better Business Bureau will not react with pleasure to today's majority decision. I would have thought that the broadcasting industry and the business community in general would want the FCC to supervise stations closely in this regard. The reputations of all stations suffer when the advertisers upon whom those stations depend for support are bilked, cheated, and defrauded through a station's illegal practices.

WIFE's admittedly fraudulent and indefensible billing practices, its conduct of the Eaton water-filter contest, its failure to show adequate supervisory control and licensee responsibility and, of great importance, the fact that the derelictions and lack of control occurred during the period of a one-year probationary grant – all are clear evidence that its license should not be permitted to continue as trustee for the public in its control of a valuable broadcast frequency. Why must this Commission, and the American public, brook the sort of corruption which has been clearly acknowledged in this case? Can the licensee's economic interests here be of such overriding importance that this Commission, on equitable grounds, must deem its further operation to be minimally in the public's interest? WIFE was given a second chance. It is not entitled to a third.

In condoning fraud in the operations of WIFE, the majority has itself deprived the public of the protection to which it is entitled.

I believe that the public is entitled to far more from the broadcasting profession and this Commission.

I dissent.

Application of Forum Communications, Inc.
17 F.C.C. 2d 959, 961,963 (1969)
Dissenting Opinion of Commissioner Nicholas Johnson

With an inspirational steadfastness of purpose, the FCC gleefully plods on today toward the cliff overhanging its coveted recognition: the award for the regulatory Commission least likely to succeed in serving the public interest.

On May 14, 1969, the attorneys for a group called Forum Communications, Inc., filed with the Commission a document entitled "Petition to Defer Action on WPIX-TV Renewal."

Thus, the Commission has been, for some time, unequivocally on notice of the intention of a citizens' group to participate in the license renewal proceeding for television station WPIX (channel 11) in New York City.

It has nonetheless built, from a scaffold of gossamer technicality, a ruling that results in the door of this public agency being firmly slammed, once again, in the face of public representatives – to serve the economic interest of one of the FCC's favored broadcast licensees.

This Commission has already rushed through its processes with extraordinary speed a protective cutoff for its broadcast licensees' renewal proceedings. ... Under the new cutoff rules, any members of the public who wish to file a competing application and participate in a station's renewal proceeding must file with us within 60 days after the renewal application has been received.

> *[O]ne is left with the uncomfortable feeling that, once again, the public has been put out of its own house.*

The notice of proposed rulemaking was published on Mar. 20, 1969. The rule was adopted on May 14, 1969. By contrast, the Commission's proposed one-to-a-market rule-making (limiting broadcast ownership to one full-time property per market) was first proposed on Mar. 27, 1968, delayed at industry request on June 3, Aug. 9, Sept. 20, 1968, and Jan. 22, 1969, and is still a long way from resolution.

Not satisfied with this prospective gift to the industry, the Commission now seeks to pass out its favors retroactively as well.

WPIX's current license expires May 31, 1969. Its new license, if granted, will take effect June 1, 1969. The Commission has the authority to perform the ministerial act of issuing the renewal prior to June 1. But there is considerable question in my mind as to our legal power to refuse to consider protesting petitions filed prior to June 1, whenever we may technically have processed or mailed out the renewal papers.

Note that this is not a case of a request for waiver of filing deadlines received after the time has expired. Forum's petition was received on May 14, a date which all would concede was long before renewals have ever been granted.

Forum could easily have filed a skeleton petition to deny renewal on that date. Had it done so, even the imaginative Broadcast Bureau would have been hard pressed to devise reasons for its unacceptability. ... Instead, Forum took the honest course. It told us in timely fashion that (a) it intended to file, (b) it would do so before June 1, and (c) it requested that we not grant the renewal prior to that time in view of our knowledge of its intentions. What could be more reasonable or straightforward?

I recognize that Forum has not followed the intricacies of our procedures to the letter. I had assumed, however, that ever since the time of the old common law writs the judicial process in most civilized nations had been liberalized somewhat.

The Commission had formerly seemed to me the Bureau of Waivers. Every Wednesday we routinely grant waivers of our rules for some (while mysteriously enforcing them for others). Ownership rules are ignored; transmitter sites are moved to create additional interference; stations held less than three years are sold; and, yes, our filing deadlines are bent well out of shape.

Indeed, at the very Commission meeting at which this infamous decision emerged the Commission announced its willingness to accept – from broadcasters only, of course – arguments and pleadings filed even after deadlines have passed! Needless to say, Forum's request is modest indeed by comparison.

No, one is left with the uncomfortable feeling that, once again, the public has been put out of its own house.

The first time we denied the public standing the U.S. Court of Appeals sent the case back to us with the stern admonition that:

> *The theory that the Commission can always effectively represent the listener interests in a renewal proceeding without the aid and participation of legitimate listener representatives fulfilling the role of private attorneys general is one of those assumptions we collectively try to work with so long as they are reasonably adequate. When it becomes clear, as it does to us now, that it is no longer a valid assumption which stands up under the realities of actual experience, neither we nor the Commission can continue to rely on it.*

Office of Communications of United Church of Christ v. FCC, 359 F. 2d 994, 1003-04 (1966) (U.S. Supreme Court Chief Justice-designate Burger writing for the Court).

Since that time we have read our rules carefully and recently found that we could provide a little carefully chosen harassment to two public petitioners by reminding them that we insist on documents that are typewritten and double spaced.

The Supreme Court of the United States commonly assists its petitioners who mistakenly choose certiorari or appeal as the route to review. It merely treats the pleading as if it were in proper form and disposes of it accordingly. It would seem to me that an administrative agency, conceived in Congressional desire to simplify legal procedure, has an obligation to do no less.

I dissent.

Addendum

Since the majority opinion and my dissent were recorded on Wednesday and released on Thursday (May 22, 1969), a number of events have occurred which warrant further comment.

Chairman Hyde has issued an opinion containing some charges which, regretfully, require reply.

Forum has filed with the Commission the petition it indicated on May 14 it would file before June 1.

Broadcast Bureau Chief George Smith has issued the license renewal for station WPIX.

It has been, in short, quite a day.

I. Chairman Hyde's Concurring Statement

Chairman Hyde has written:

Commissioner Johnson sought to have the orderly renewal of a broadcast station license deferred so that a competing application could be filed; and now, having failed in obtaining agreement for that purpose, he attacks the integrity of the other members of the Commission and accuses the Agency of proceeding in a manner contrary to accepted legal procedure.

I have not, in this case or any other since my term began on July 1, 1966, ever sought to have the orderly renewal of a broadcast station license deferred so that a competing application could be filed. As I noted, the majority expressly instructed the Chief of the Broadcast Bureau to follow the regular and normal procedure. Chairman Hyde repeats in his opinion today that the renewal in question is to be processed in the normal and ordinary course of Commission business. As we shall shortly see, the Broadcast Bureau has pointedly flouted this instruction. But I think my opinion makes clear that I would have been perfectly willing to abide the majority's judgment on this issue. Indeed, that's what the controversy was all about. It seemed to me that Forum was, in fact, asking for no more than normal and ordinary course of Commission business would have given it anyway (namely, that the renewal would not be granted until the end of the month), and that it was entitled to it as a matter of law and good administrative practice. I did attempt to obtain agreement for the position expressed in my dissent, as I generally do on matters before the Commission. I felt then, and in light of recent events feel even more strongly now, that such would have been a more prudent course for this Commission to follow.

I regret that Chairman Hyde feels there is something involved in this case, or in my opinion, that raises an issue in his mind as to the integrity of the Commissioners. I have often praised my colleagues publicly, including Chairman Hyde. We have occasionally disagreed on the results in cases, and the reasons for those results. But I have never – certainly never intentionally – engaged in *ad hominem* arguments or hinted at any lack of personal integrity. I do not do so now and would not. I can only operate on the assumption – backed by my personal experience – that my colleagues are men of experience, ability, and integrity who are required by law to express their personal, honestly arrived at (and occasionally conflicting) views on the cases before this Commission.

Chairman Hyde goes on to say:

An agency that is charged with proceeding in an adjudicatory manner in its licensing responsibility must not engage in actively encouraging the filing of competing applications lest it finds itself prejudiced toward existing licensees. The renewal in question is to be processed in the normal and ordinary course of Commission business. Had a majority of the Commissioners decided to hold up the renewal until such time as another applicant could file on top of it, we certainly could stand accused of soliciting competing applicants in a manner contrary to the interest and spirit of the Communications Act.

There is absolutely nothing in this paragraph with which I take exception – except its relevance to the matter at hand.

We were presented with a legal document by a citizens group. We were required to dispose of it. I felt we should grant it; the majority of the Commission disagreed. To have granted it could not possibly have been interpreted as soliciting competing applicants or actively encouraging the filing of competing applications. We would have been simply actively disposing of applications already filed, not encouraging their filing.

The mere suggestion of encouraging or soliciting competing applications is loaded with political and emotional dynamite at this point in history, as Chairman Hyde is aware. We spent two days before the Senate Commerce Committee and one day before the Communications Subcommittee of the House Interstate and Foreign Commerce Committee on March 4-6 of this year. Each of the Commissioners provided assurances at that time that they had not, and would not, actively solicit competing applications for stations. I am prepared to repeat those assurances today, as, I have little doubt, could each of the other Commissioners. To suggest that any of us has been a party to the deferral of orderly renewal, or that we have been actively encouraging, hold[ing] up the renewal, or soliciting competing applicants in a manner contrary to the interest and spirit of the Communications Act is, most charitably, misleading.

II. Forum's Filing and the WPIX License Renewal

As of this writing my sole source of information as to the events of yesterday (Thursday, May 22, 1969) is a story in this morning's *New York Times*. The *Times* reports that Forum filed sometime yesterday the pleading it earlier indicated to the Commission it would file by June 1. It also reports, referring to Broadcast Bureau Chief George Smith as a source, that the WPIX renewal was granted sometime yesterday.

[T]he Broadcast Bureau publicly announced its renewals of broadcast station licenses due February 1 and April 1 of this year (they are processed in batches every two months of the year) after those dates, not before. Thus, the public announcement of the WPIX renewal on May 22 – more than a week prior to June 1 – would appear to be rather significantly earlier than normal.

The Commission said in its order of yesterday that the WPIX renewal would follow the regular and normal procedure. Chairman Hyde repeats in his statement of today that the renewal in question is to be processed in the normal and ordinary course of Commission business. Whatever else may be said of the Broadcast Bureau's actions it is clear these directions have not been complied with.

I trust we will be hearing more of this matter. It is regrettable.

Applications of National Broadcasting Co.
16 F.C.C.2d 698 (1969)
Dissenting Opinion of Commissioner Nicholas Johnson

The NBC-owned stations in California (KNBC-TV, Los Angeles; KNBR-AM-FM, San Francisco) were due for renewal December 1, 1968. Their renewal has been deferred for several months because of unresolved matters concerning the qualification of NBC as a licensee. KNBC-TV had a competing application filed against it on February 4, 1969, which has not yet been resolved. Today the majority nevertheless renews the NBC radio stations in San Francisco, KNBR-AM and KNBR-FM. I dissent.

My most fundamental concern is that NBC — chastised several times by this Commission and notified that the matters would be considered at renewal — can have licenses for multimillion-dollar operations renewed without any real Commission scrutiny. A small, family-owned AM radio station that operates with the wrong power for a few days, or comes on the air before sunup, may be levied a substantial fine by this Commission. Time brokerage, false logging, or an abuse of advertisers — such as double billing — may actually result in license revocation. And yet this Commission is unwilling even to review the case against NBC, and simply

The Commission's actions will serve to demonstrate [its] double standard when it comes to dealing with its powerful licensees in contrast to the treatment of family-owned AM radio stations guilty of minor infractions.

acquiesces in the renewal of these two profitable licenses. It makes no review of NBC responses to previously expressed Commission concern. Although the majority has prepared a formal order there is nothing to explain why the majority, despite previous admonishments to NBC, now finds renewal to be in the public interest. It is a well-established principle that renewal time is an occasion for review of the past behavior of the licensee seeking renewal. But recent Commission action regarding NBC is ignored.

A review of the Commission's actions will serve to demonstrate the majority's dereliction in this matter – and the Commission's double standard when it comes to dealing with its powerful licensees in contrast to the treatment of family-owned AM radio stations guilty of minor infractions.

(1) On May 1, 1968 the Commission wrote NBC concerning "allegations that your broadcasts of the 'Hollywood Golden Globe Awards' have contained substantial misrepresentations." The Commission, after investigation, concluded:

[We] believe that your "Golden Globe Award" broadcasts prior to 1968 substantially misled the public as to the basis on which winners were chosen and the procedures followed in choosing them, and that you were seriously delinquent in this respect … .

We believe that you have fallen far below the degree of responsibility which is expected of a licensee with respect to the matters set forth herein, and we request that you submit a statement as to future procedures to be followed with respect to this program and other programs raising comparable problems. This matter will be considered further in connection with the next application for renewal of license of your Los Angeles television station, KNBC.

(2) On October 9, 1968, the Commission wrote NBC concerning procedures on two of its quiz-game shows – "PDQ" and "Hollywood Squares." The Commission concluded:

[The] public has from time to time been misled as to the procedures preceding the questioning of guest celebrities on "Hollywood Squares," and that your own procedures for prevention of improper practices on these programs has been lax.

The matters set forth above will be considered further in connection with the pending application for renewal of license of station KNBC.

The plain language of these letters would seem to indicate further Commission study would be warranted when the KNBC renewal was considered. NBC apparently thought the matters serious since its president wrote Chairman Hyde a seven-page letter concerning "our exercise of supervision over game and award shows." But there is not one word regarding these matters in the majority opinion renewing the stations' licenses.

(3) The Commission has received numerous complaints regarding NBC's coverage of the 1968 Democratic National Convention. Those matters have not yet been finally disposed of by the Commission.

(4) One of the charges against NBC in connection with its coverage of the Democratic Convention was the allegation that NBC employees had placed a hidden microphone in a room that was subsequently used for closed platform committee hearings.

Is there no possibility that a resolution of these charges might reflect adversely on NBC as a licensee seeking renewal?

(5) On September 11, 1968, the Commission wrote NBC concerning possible conflicts of interest

involving one of its commentators, Chet Huntley – and his comments about regulation involving meat inspection. The Commission noted:

> [We] find that NBC did not exercise reasonable diligence in light of information publicly available and information brought to its attention ... .
>
> The above record over the period stretching from 1964 to the present shows a failure to exercise reasonable diligence or to fulfill public interest requirements in this important area.
>
> Thus, you appear to have fallen short of your responsibilities with respect to the matters set forth with regard to the fairness doctrine.

There is no mention of this matter in any Commission consideration of these renewals despite the fact that NBC submitted an eight-page response on October 21, 1968. Needless to say, no Commission evaluation of that response has been made nor follow-up undertaken.

(6) On September 17, 1968, the Commission wrote NBC concerning a "Lucky Bucks" contest presented over NBC station WKYC in Cleveland, Ohio. The Commission concluded:

> In the Eastern Broadcasting Corp. letter the Commission noted that advertising deception may result from the use of statements which are not technically false or which may even be literally true, since the only relevant consideration is the impact of the statements on the general public, including the ignorant, the unthinking, and the credulous. Applying this proposition to the instant case, the Commission is of the view that the

advertisements pertaining to the WKYC "Million Dollar" contest tended to mislead the public in that they contained extravagant claims concerning the amount of money to be given away.

In view of all the circumstances of this matter, the Commission is of the opinion that the advertising pertaining to the WKYC "Million Dollar" contest fell short of the required degree of licensee responsibility. This matter will be considered further in connection with the next applications for renewal of license of stations WKYC-AM-FM.

(The majority referred to the Eastern Broadcasting Corp. case. In that case Eastern Broadcasting's license renewal was limited to a one-year period for station WCVS, Springfield Ill., because of a "Lucky Bucks" contest. The Commission learned of the NBC-WKYC contest only because part of Eastern's defense was that it simply duplicated a contest being run by the Cleveland, Ohio, NBC radio stations.) If today's action is any indication, the promise to consider the misleading "Lucky Bucks" contest with the WKYC renewals is not worth the paper it is printed on.

(7) In March 1968 the Commission considered reports in a Los Angeles newspaper that a KNBC-TV crew had brought "dove" and "hawk" picket signs for use in filming a student debate at Claremont College (in the Los Angeles area). NBC responded that the signs had been prepared "to depict 'sloganeering' as opposed to the type of mature debate shown on the program, or merely as colorful additions to the set." The Commission disposed of this matter without further

action in a Minute entry for March 20, 1968, with Commissioner Cox issuing a concurring statement joined in by Commissioners Wadsworth and Johnson.

The slogans were "Victory in Viet Nam," "No Retreat," "Stop Communism," "End the Bombing," "Down with the Draft," and "Bring Them Home." The *Los Angeles Times* reported that the students complained that the signs would misrepresent student feeling on the issue and began to picket the NBC cameramen with their own signs that read "Hearst is alive and working at NBC." It also reported that the start of the debate was delayed while students heckled the NBC crew and that both speakers in the debate criticized the TV men for bringing the signs.

(8) Finally, the corporate structure of RCA has changed substantially since the last NBC renewals. RCA has acquired St. Regis Paper Co., a $700-million transaction, "its largest acquisition to date." St. Regis Paper, with its wood products, packaging, paper, forestry, and timberland (7.5-million acres), food processing, and manufacture of ice skating and curling rinks is to be added to RCA-NBC's other acquisitions in electronics, publications (*e.g.*, Random House) and consumer services (*e.g.*, Hertz).

The concern about conglomerate acquisitions expressed by experts versed in study of the functioning of the American economy is well known. Normally the FCC dodges the question unless license transfers are before it. Now even this Commission has expressed the need to examine the conglomerate influence in broadcasting in its *Inquiry into the Ownership of Broadcast Stations by Persons or Entities with Other*

Business Interests. But does not a license renewal imply that nothing has occurred to warrant further evaluation and study? How can this Commission renew NBC licenses without even giving cursory examination to the most recent, and largest acquisition in RCA's history? And yet, this it declines to do.

Since the preparation of this opinion there have been news reports that St. Regis Paper Co. has terminated the merger agreement. The question of St. Regis' relationship to the RCA-NBC knowledge industry conglomerate thus may be moot – but this does not detract from the fact that the majority was apparently willing to go on granting RCA-NBC applications without even examining the impact of RCA's largest acquisition.

Based on preliminary analysis of newspaper reports there would be several issues that could have been explored by this Commission: (1) What will be the financial impact of this merger on RCA-NBC, especially in terms of profit and cash flow positions? Will there be increased pressure on NBC to meet deficit cash flow problems in the first years after the St. Regis acquisition? (2) What is the future relationship of St. Regis to the other knowledge components of the RCA-NBC conglomerate, *e.g.,* Random House? (3) What is the relationship (present and future) of St. Regis as a supplier to RCA-NBC competitors (newspapers, magazines, book publishers) and, RCA-NBC affiliates (newspapers, magazines, book publishers owning broadcast stations affiliated with NBC) and, to owners of broadcast station affiliates in competition with NBC affiliates?

At the time of writing the exact status of this merger – and certainly the answers to these questions – remains in doubt.

All these incidents, whether drawn from radio or television, raise the issue of the suitability of RCA-NBC, a powerful corporate conglomerate and communications entity with numerous radio and television outlets, to be a broadcast licensee. The FCC must find that the public interest will be served by renewal of these NBC licenses. And it is only at the time of renewal of individual licenses that the past behavior of RCA-NBC can be evaluated. The majority concedes that it has "not in this order undertaken to dispose of complaints against other NBC stations," and declares its intention to dispose of them in "other proceedings." It is very difficult to conjure up just what kind of "other proceedings" the majority may have in mind if they are not to be license renewal proceedings on NBC-owned stations. The complaints are not directed against "stations," but against the licensee: RCA/NBC. And it is precisely in the renewal proceeding now before us that NBC's qualifications as a licensee are in issue and that we must find this renewal will serve the public interest. If the issues are not to be dealt with now, when will they ever be considered?

It was expected that the evaluation of the alleged violations enumerated above – some of which involved KNBC-TV – could be made in the context of the first NBC renewal, that of KNBC-TV. That action has been deferred. The licenses now before us are for radio stations in San Francisco, and these are the first NBC renewal applications to be approved since the alleged incidents occurred. For the majority to find that the public interest will be served by renewal of these NBC stations while conceding the need for additional proceedings regarding this licensee's performance is simply incredible. And the individual stations involved are really irrelevant. What is relevant is that the only opportunity to review the licensee responsibility and performance of a corporate conglomerate network with owned and operated stations is at the renewal of its broadcast properties – the first renewals after the behavior in question. This the majority refuses to do here – refusing even to mention all the incidents I have detailed in its order granting renewal.

> *This Commission weekly imposes monetary fines on licensees, and even issues short-term renewals, for behavior less serious than these seven incidents regarding NBC.*

The recitation of these matters has been lengthy. Perhaps it is mere coincidence that over a five-month period NBC was involved in seven separate instances in which the licensee apparently fell short of meeting its responsibilities in supervision of program production, employee behavior, or advertising practices. But perhaps it indicates more, a general laxness on NBC's part.

This Commission weekly imposes monetary fines on licensees, and even issues short-term renewals, for behavior less serious than these seven incidents regarding NBC. For the majority not even formally to review the NBC record in an order or letter suggests an unconscionable double standard. The three California Pacifica stations have been deferred for as long as the NBC California stations. The reason for deferring the Pacifica stations – including the one-time, early-morning-hours broadcast of an allegedly obscene record, brought to our attention by no one save *Broadcasting* magazine – is a matter the Broadcast Bureau now concedes was unwise. One is forced to the conclusion that politically weak, financially precarious Commission licensees feel the full force of Commission wrath while the rich and powerful remain immune.

I dissent.

Chapter Ten
A Day in the Life: The Federal Communications Commission
82 Yale L.J. 1575-1634 (1973)

Introduction. *Near the end of my seven-year-plus term my team and I became increasingly aware of the limitations of dissenting opinions in selected individual cases to communicate to the Congress, media and public the systemic failings of the FCC. Perhaps, we thought, an article explaining why every item on a weekly Wednesday meeting agenda was wrongly considered and decided would better make the point – in effect a dissenting opinion to everything the FCC does. Wednesday, December 13, 1972, was selected at random. This 60-page Yale Law Journal article was the result. Given its length, only its opening and conclusion are included in this chapter.*
The entire article can be found on my Web site, nicholasjohnson.org, in hardcopy at law libraries, and from commercial electronic services. (a) Reading about each item and why we thought it was wrongly decided is still interesting, to some degree insightful, and occasionally even amusing. But it is primarily made available for other reasons: (b) the insights it may provide students and professors of administrative law into the overall workload and processes of at least this one agency on one day, (c) an overview for students of communications or mass media law of the structure and function of the FCC (as of 1973) insofar as it affected the evolution of FCC broadcasting and cable

policy and regulation, and (d) an interesting slice of broadcasting history.
The article reflects the opinion and experience of one FCC Commissioner and is written in the first person. However, it represents the work of many people. The contribution of John Jay Dystel, a legal assistant, was sufficient to credit him as a co-author. I was also assisted in the preparation of the weekly agenda by my permanent office manager and economic and legal assistant, Robert S. Thorpe, and my other legal assistant during the 1972-1973 term, Larry S. Gage. The idea of a dissent to an entire Commission agenda was initially discussed with Tracy A. Westen, a legal assistant during the 1969-1970 term. My assistant, Mary Ann Tsucalas, provided her usual professional editorial assistance and manuscript production. – Nicholas Johnson, May 2019

For seven years I have struggled with the FCC in an effort to inject some rationality into its decision-making process and to reveal its workings to the public. There is reason enough to assert that everything the FCC does is wrong. But, like contributions to the literature detailing disasters in given areas of Commission responsibility, such assertions are almost universally dismissed as exaggerations.

And so it is that I have come to try to describe the agency one more time, but from a unique perspective: "A day in the life" of the Federal Communications Commission. The day – Wednesday, December 13, 1972 – was selected from the Commission's meeting days in 1972. It is neither better nor worse than any other day during the past seven years. It is typical. This article is an effort to describe what the FCC did on that typical Wednesday.

Professors and students of administrative law tend to concentrate on a particular agency decision – usually one that has gone to the appellate courts. But a look at one day's events may well be more instructive than a close examination of a single event in determining why an agency is failing at its job or why it acts in a consistently unprincipled manner.

The seven FCC Commissioners meet weekly, on Wednesdays, to vote on the items brought to their attention by the Commission's various bureaus. It is not clear who decides what matters will be considered. The agenda is the product of industry pressures, staff idiosyncrasies, and political judgments. If he or she chooses, however, the Chair is in a position to control the flow of items to the Commission.

Most matters are not handled at FCC meetings but are delegated by the Commission to the staff for action. In theory these items are in areas of settled Commission policy but, in fact, the Commission has not so limited the scope of its delegations. During my term the majority has been unwilling to examine its delegation orders or to enunciate what standards control the delegation of decision-making authority.

Those issues which do reach the Commissioners each week often take them by surprise. Opening a new agenda (the stack of mimeographed staff memos and accompanying recommended opinions for a Wednesday meeting) is like Christmas morning. All too often the agenda includes a long, detailed staff document dealing with a controversial and complicated matter in which: (1) numerous alternatives are presented (or excluded) after extensive staff work, (2) the proposed resolution is endorsed by all of the Commission's bureau chiefs, (3) an immediate decision is required, and (4) any alteration in the proposed resolution will mean considerably more staff work and costly delay. As a result, rational decision-making suffers.

On December 13, 1972, the Commission was presented with fifty-nine items. In each case the staff made a recommendation to the Commissioners. If a majority votes to approve the staff's recommendation it adopts the proposed Commission opinion as well. If one of the Commissioners questions a particular item, there is a discussion with the staff prior to a vote. On December 13, twenty-eight of the fifty-nine items were discussed.

Each week's agenda is divided into thirteen substantive categories [followed by pages in the *Yale Law Journal* article where the week's items are discussed]: Hearing [pp. 1579-1581], General [pp. 1582-1589], Safety and Special [pp. 1589-1590], Common Carrier [pp. 1590-1594], Personnel [pp. 1594-1595], Classified [pp. 1595], CATV [pp. 1595-1599], Assignment and Transfer [pp. 1599-1604]. Renewals [pp. 1604-1608], Aural [pp. 1609-1613], Television [pp1613-1617], Broadcast [pp. 1617-1623], and Complaints and Compliance [pp. 1623-1632] – in that order.

Conclusion

Ten years ago I came to Washington as an administrative law professor to find out more about administrative process. A seven-year appointment to the FCC in 1966 has given me more administrative experience than I bargained for and left me with a conviction that administrative law students and professors need more of the raw data on actual agency operation than currently is available. This article is an attempt to provide some of that material.

Several conclusions emerge.

First, it seems evident that the FCC deals each week with an incredibly broad range of communications matters. On December 13, the FCC considered everything from personnel decisions to significant issues of international consequence. The Commission delved into areas surely beyond its expertise and into issues simply beyond its ken.

Second, as the Hearing Agenda reveals, the Commission, burdened with so much work and having so few resources, takes years to resolve important cases.

Third, as both the Cable and Aural Agendas illustrate, the FCC is manipulated daily by the industries it is supposed to regulate and by its own staff. As a result the Commissioners often make precedents which return to haunt them.

Fourth, if the FCC no longer approves of its own rules and precedents, it simply ignores them – either by waiving them to death or otherwise evading them. In short, the concept of principled decision-making does not exist at the FCC.

Fifth, the FCC not only disdains its own administrative principles, but it also ignores those established by the judiciary. Thus, on December 13 the FCC simply turned its back on numerous decisions construing the National Environmental Policy Act (1970) and relied on a construction of a recent case involving programming "format changes" not justified by the language of that case.

Sixth, as the General and Common Carrier Agendas show especially well, the Commissioners often decide cases they do not understand.

Finally, the Commission has not developed rational communications policies for governing its day-to-day decisions.

Perhaps it is easier to understand the Commission's sloppy work, its serious gaffs, when one sees an individual decision in the context of the burdensome "day in the life" on which it was voted. Yet much of the burden is of the Commission's own making. It is neither necessary nor advisable to divide up the FCC's workload between a "Broadcasting Commission" and a "Communications Common Carrier Commission." First semester business school principles would suggest that the Commission should formulate some statements of national communications policy for the benefit of itself, its staff, the business community, the Congress, the press, and the public. Having done this, it should prepare precise delegation orders to its staff, allow the staff to handle individual cases as they come up, and create a management information reporting system whereby the Commissioners are able to follow the processing of cases, modifying policy and delegation orders as warranted.

Another purpose of this piece is to offer the public some information concerning the operation of one of its administrative agencies, one which has struggled to keep its activities secret. The FCC is a public agency, receiving public funds for the purpose of regulating, "in the public interest," communications industries whose services are crucial to the continued vitality of a democratic society. Ironically, though the agency keeps the public in the dark, the communications interests learn all the details of Commission actions through information services provided by lawyers, lobbyists, and the trade press.

Neither the Commission majority nor its staff is troubled by the agency's treatment of the public. Whether because they adhere to notions of laissez-faire economics or because they sympathize with communications industry interests, a majority of the staff at the FCC exploit the lack of public representation day after day.

Congress has done little to correct problems so apparent at the FCC largely because, as a generalist and political body subject to the same sorts of pressures that barrage the Commission, Congress is not terribly competent to supervise.

A final purpose of this article, then, is to offer the judicial branch some idea of how bad things really are, of how tenuous is the basis for the idea that judges should defer to the FCC's "rational and orderly process." Long-range reforms aside, if there is to be any immediate hope for the FCC, it lies with the courts.

230 – Catfish Solution

Chapter Eleven
The Way Out: Some Proposals for Reform

It Is no accident that you have now seen the FCC from every conceivable perspective. Actual cases were provided, the legal documents were reprinted, rather than leaving the details to my selective recollection and the analysis to my Monday morning quarterbacking. I did not want the book open to the criticism that the examples and analyses put the worst possible light on the Commission's work product.

Lest the suspicion surface that the routine cases chosen may not have merited the agency's best effort, there was also an analysis of the largest, most consequential merger of broadcast properties in the FCC's history. For those who believe a more exhaustive review of a given area of Commission activity would be the fairest evaluation, there was an examination of the license renewal process. Finally, if you believe the depiction of Commission broadcast regulation atypical there is the "A Day in the Life" report of an entire day's work product — perhaps the fairest random sampling of all.

If I have been successful in my efforts you should now be close to screaming, "All right, already, it's terrible! I agree with you. Something must be done about the Federal Communications Commission."

We have seen a pervasive anti-intellectualism in an organization that ought to think of itself as a think tank headed by seven of Plato's philosopher kings.

FCC Commissioners are paid, and quite adequately, to *think* about the wisest communications policies for our nation. If they don't do it not only are they derelict in their duties, there is no one else with the resources and power to do the job for them. The chaotic consequences for our nation include a negative economic impact of multi-billion-dollar proportions and unmeasured human havoc.

There is little knowledge, interest, or enthusiasm for management or administration at the FCC. There is a reluctance to undertake anything that might be characterized as research and development, systems analysis, or policy studies. There is not even much commitment to precedent – to following today what you said yesterday would guide you – or the notion that decisions should be accompanied by *some* rational, logical progression of analysis as to why they were made. There is little talk or apparent concern for the dictates of the national interest, little sense of responsibility for the untold millions who, if they were to think about the matter at all, would look to the Commission to represent them.

And pervading all is what comes to be characterized as "industry capture" of the agency. Large corporate interests tend to come away from the FCC with what it is they came to get – unless, of course, they are opposed by other large interests. Such occasional punishments as are meted out tend to fall hardest upon those least able to sustain them – the small mom-and-pop radio stations, for example, instead of the multi-million-dollar television stations owned by the networks. Those who seek to represent consumers, American citizens challenging FCC actions, are met with hostile resistance from the FCC at every turn – so serious that the U.S. Court of Appeals has often found the agency in violation of law, not to mention propriety.

The concept of subgovernment has been offered as one explanation for the FCC's performance.

Yet the questions remain of what we can do about it.

The answer is that there are a good many things that can be done, whether an occasional letter by an unsophisticated citizen with full-time commitments elsewhere, professional efforts of a young lawyer with a reformer's zeal, a station employee with a guilty conscience, an ambitious reporter, an elected official or an FCC commissioner. Good government is the business of all of us in a democracy, something we all have the power and opportunity to affect in some way. The Watergates of Washington – and there's an expose every day for the reporter who'll look for it – are monuments to our neglect.

The difficulty comes when trying to break through the vicious circle. What are the elements contributing to our challenge?

The quality of the commissioners affects the quality of staff they choose – Commission staff (about 2,000 employees), personal staff (about six per Commissioner) – and quality of management they provide.

The quality of commissioners is, in turn, a function of the selection process of the president, and

U.S. senators' standards for confirmation of presidential nominees.

The choice of commissioners is a function of history and tradition; willingness of persons to serve; personal idealism, interest and imagination of the president; political power and pressure of the broadcasting industry, senators and others seeking political patronage; effectiveness of citizen groups; and willingness of mass media to make news, and therefore a political issue, out of the appointments.

The colloquium form of administration has strengths. The seven independent commissioners are responsible neither to each other nor any other individual in government. Ideally that would enable a greater wisdom to emerge from spirited inquiry and debate by the group than would come from a single agency head, such as the Maritime Administrator at the Maritime Administration.

Consensus, while possible, is not mandated. Each commissioner has not only the opportunity but the responsibility to express separate and dissenting views. It is a function related to that of an inspector general, internal auditor, or ombudsperson. Public dissent provides a peephole into the dusty process that is not available in executive branch agencies, the military, or corporate enterprises, and a tremendous advantage to Congress, press, academic community, and interested citizens. There is always the possibility that wiser decisions will be arrived at as a result of the group's deliberations and diverse points of view. And there is a check on dictatorial control of anything as potentially powerful as regulation of radio and television in a free society.

But it also has the disadvantage of any group effort: its horses resemble camels. Even with seven equally intelligent, conscientious and energetic commissioners, the task of getting four or five of them to agree to follow a given course of action long enough to get anything accomplished is not an easy one. If there are commissioners with strong differences of philosophy, excessive commitments to industry points of view, or relative lack of interest in the business at hand, it makes concerted effort almost impossible.

> *The FCC simply hasn't the staff or the political goodies to compete with industry lobbying, questions of propriety would be raised if it did, and it rarely has the will. There is no citizens' lobby to counter the industry, and it generally wins by default.*

Even assuming a high quality of commissioners and their agreed-upon course of action, there is the countervailing power of the regulated industries. The Commission has rarely proposed even modest efforts at broadcast regulation. But on those few occasions when it has – Chairman Bill Henry's effort to adopt the industry's own standards for commercial content in programs, denial of a license for WHDH-TV in Boston, or the seemingly pro-broadcasting cable television rules – the industry has swarmed around Capitol Hill like flies to a barnyard manure pile. Campaign contributions and free radio and television news coverage are offered incumbents. Distorted versions of the FCC's proposed action are pressed upon senators and House members and their staffs.

The FCC simply hasn't the staff or the political goodies to compete with industry lobbying, questions of propriety would be raised if it did, and it rarely has the will. There is no citizens' lobby to counter the industry, and it generally wins by default.

The circle fades to black. The subgovernment, like mold, grows best in the dark. Every institution in America needs the disinfectant of the media's sunlight. The regulatory commissions have little or none, aside from their subgovernment's sycophantic, industry-limited-circulation trade press.

There are thousands of media employees in Washington. Unfortunately, many are told to be what I call repeaters rather than reporters. They attend press conferences, pick at the sandwiches and press releases, and distribute throughout the country what government officials want repeated; thus earning a living for themselves, saving on food bills, and avoiding for the agencies what would otherwise be enormous advertising, printing, and distribution costs. Like sparrows sunning themselves on a country telephone wire, and irrationally but urgently following a leader to another wire three feet away, the Washington press corps moves like a pack from the White House to the Pentagon to the State Department to Capitol Hill and back again.

It may provide more pay and excitement than wearing a path from the mayor's office to police blotter to hospital emergency room in the cause of local news, but it's not my idea of reporting. Meanwhile, the country's top 500 corporations and subgovernments they support are robbing the taxpayer and consumer blind in collaboration with the regulatory commissions and executive branch agencies set up to regulate them. That story is seldom even explored let alone reported.

There are many reasons for the failure to cover the regulatory commissions. For now it's sufficient to note the consequences. Rarely do elected or appointed public officials pay much of a price for going along with industry; few get any advantage or credit for resisting.

When President Nixon goes to China, or President Gerald Ford personally toasts an English muffin, they are praised; when Nixon commits impeachable offenses, or Ford pardons Nixon for them, they are criticized. But when a president appoints an industry hack to a regulatory commission, invites corporate broadcasting executives to a private White House dinner, or tells them he'll support a license renewal bill, little notice is paid. Nor do they get much credit for vetoing a piece of pro-industry legislation, slashing a corporate subsidy budget item, or appointing a bright consumer advocate to an agency. The same results befall senators, members of Congress, and FCC commissioners.

A modest regulatory proposal will produce loud, shrill cries from an industry in discomfort. It is unlikely there will be any editorial comment in support. A totally irrational Commission opinion, with or without dissent, will go largely unnoticed. An industry protection measure may prompt campaign contributions and a round of golf at Congressional Country Club. But it is unlikely to threaten a senator or commissioner with hostile questioning from the press.

The Supreme Court is at least subjected to a footnote-by-footnote analysis of its opinions in a few dozen academic law reviews, and a broad-brush treatment of its major opinions in the general press by a handful of competent reporters. Regulatory commissions' opinions are largely ignored by even the academic community, let alone the general press.

It is unlikely we will simultaneously have quality commissioners and staff, an interested and idealistic president, a responsible and independent Senate and House, and a tough investigative press corps. On the other hand, it is difficult to improve the situation without improving all these elements.

There may be thoroughgoing theoretical solutions to this dilemma. But the only practical solutions occurring to me so far come down to an old Iowa adage about a city cousin's visit to the farm. Looking around and asking what she might do to help, she was told to "grab a plow and start plowing." In other words, do what you can; know the problems and the pressure points; get as many people involved as possible; and work in all arenas at once.

Appointments. Consider, for example, the first factor discussed: the quality of the commissioners. There are (or have been) commissioners who drink too much, sleep during oral arguments, demonstrate by their questions (or their silence) that they have little interest in or knowledge of the subject at hand, have neither convictions nor the courage to express them, work only two or three days a week, spend most of their time with industry representatives, are lacking in the minimal intellectual skills necessary to formulate economic and social policy, are petty and mean toward their enemies and unjustifiably generous with their friends. The least that can be said is such persons make it more difficult for the FCC to conduct its business in the public interest.

Seven bright, tough, able, independent, responsible, professional, conscientious commissioners serving at the same time could work wonders. Note there's no mention of liberal or radical, nor need they be brilliant or intellectual. It is unreasonable to expect a covey of superstars for a lowly agency like the FCC. But are normal, decent human beings with some minimal skills for the job they are to fill too much to ask?

Some modest minimum requirements might be that:

(1) commissioners not come from the industries they are supposed to regulate, not have a desire to be reappointed through the influence of those industries, or be hired by them when leaving;

(2) have a lively curiosity about social policy issues and regular contact with books;

(3) have the judicial or scientific restraint to withhold judgment while awaiting the facts, and change deeply-held views when warranted;

(4) have a sense of commitment to all the American people, a sense of awe and responsibility

about public office as something more than a stepping-stone to private gain; and

(5) have the ability and courage to speak up, vote, and act on their convictions regardless of unpopularity with their colleagues, industry, the president or Congress.

Much of a nation's ability to obtain such public servants is a function of custom and expectations. In England a small Ditchley Conference focused on judicial review of administrative agencies. Chief Justice Warren Burger and other notables were in attendance from the United States and our counterparts were there from England. We dropped in on randomly selected proceedings in London and then later repeated the study in the United States.

The quality of administrators the British had working on the lowliest of conflicts was impressive. One case involved a tenant who was being evicted because of her failure to tend to a problem brought about by her large number of cats and small number of infrequently changed kitty litter boxes. For this tenant, and presumably others living in the building, the conflict was serious. But for the hearing examiner – who was paid little or nothing, impeccably dressed, eloquent of speech, probably possessed of an Oxford or Cambridge degree and family wealth – it was scarcely the highest calling to which he might aspire. America does not fare well when one compares this man's qualifications with those of individuals President Richard Nixon has proposed for our Supreme Court.

A part of the reason for the differences is that the rich and well educated in England have a sense of public citizenship and service. The Prime Minister would not hesitate to ask a highly qualified person to resolve a dispute or sit on a board of inquiry. In the United States it is not uncommon for someone to decline public service on grounds they "cannot afford the cut in salary" to the $30,000 to $60,000 a year now paid many in federal service. Imagine what they'd say if asked to serve without pay!

In this country, public scorn is not heaped upon someone who takes inherited wealth and the finest education and squanders it on personal pleasures and efforts to attain further riches beyond their wildest dreams of avarice. That's the great American way.

It would be helpful if press and public made more of an issue of who is appointed to regulatory commissions. Because appointments are generally for statutory terms it is easy to know when they are coming up. The White House should hear from voters at that time. If there's no short list of names, a general appeal to appoint consumer advocates could be useful. Citizens' lobby groups should make appointments an issue. Such appointments are generally checked with industry trade associations for comment (or veto). Why shouldn't citizen and consumer groups insist upon equivalent participation? Such groups are in a position to study those named in the trade press as possible nominees and propose their own lists of names.

There should be a broader cross-section of the American people serving as commissioners and members of advisory committees. We have now elevated our consciousness to recognize that Blacks and women have been systematically excluded. What of the elderly, the poor, young people, blue collar workers, housewives and other major segments of our population? Why should they be totally unrepresented? We should encourage the expectation of public service from all our citizens, not just war resisters, and not just for two years. Professions other than lawyers should be tapped. Why should it be unheard of for a public-spirited doctor to forgo a $150,000-a-year practice for a term on the Civil Aeronautics Board? He or she would undoubtedly bring as much or more sense of public responsibility, and even airline expertise, to the agency as many of the commissioners who have served there during the past decade. The scientific and medical knowledge they would bring could be of peripheral applicability in many agencies. The same could be said for all the professions and trades.

The president is often stymied when looking for people to appoint. No president will consistently follow the lead of consumer groups merely because they participate. But such groups could provide White House staff names of persons worth serious consideration.

Senators should be reminded by their constituents that if the Senate continues to vote lackluster industry lapdogs onto regulatory commissions their constituents may start voting qualified consumer advocates into the U.S. Senate.

More media coverage of this process would be somewhere between helpful and essential in making it more democratic. It borders on fraud to give the public an impression the U.S. government consists of little more than a president, secretary of state, and a handful of presidential contenders in the Senate. Essential to that task is coverage of regulatory commissioner appointments, if not in depth, then at least in the simplistic terms of pro-consumer vs. pro-industry, and competent vs. hack.

Congress. The role of the Congress is central to reform of the FCC. Members of Congress and senators are involved in its processes in so many ways. Every school child knows that Congress passes laws, and therefore laws affecting broadcasting and FCC regulation.

But the Communications Act of 1934 is still the agency's basic charter. Major congressional revisions in agency legislation seldom occur more than once a generation. That is not to make light of the legislative process. Many of the amendments to the 1934 Act have had significant impact; the bill requiring television sets to have UHF-receiving capability or the bill establishing the Public Broadcasting Corporation are but two examples. And when a major overhaul does come along, it is essential that industry lobbyists be challenged. My point is that legislation is only a small part of Congressional participation.

The budget process involves the lifeblood of any agency. Congress can increase or decrease any budget item or overall appropriation. When Maritime Administrator, this meant total control of my agency's substantive programs as well as administrative activities. How many ships we built, how many lines we subsidized, was wholly a function of the whims of the House Appropriations Committee (which took a special interest in the agency and generally urged me to spend more money than the President or I thought wise). The

House Merchant Marine and Fisheries Committee, which the casual observer would assume had primary authority over the agency, had much less impact in fact.

In the case of the FCC or the other regulatory commissions, the appropriations process has little effect on multi-million-dollar substantive programs because there are no such programs. A couple ships at the Maritime Administration cost more than the entire FCC budget. The FCC has no massive funds for research and development, nor does it construct and operate communications facilities.

The Minister of Posts and Telecommunications in some countries not only exercises functions similar to those of our FCC, but also operates the post office, telegraph company, telephone company, and public broadcasting system. The budget for such a ministry would be more comparable to that of the Maritime Administration.

Nonetheless, even though the FCC's budget is mostly salaries for personnel the Appropriations Committee has an enormous role in determining its programs. At one time the FCC had but three investigators who traveled in pairs to investigate some 60,000 complaints throughout the country. The Complaints and Compliance Bureau Chief, Bill Ray, one of the Commission's most conscientious, able and hardworking employees, would have liked a little more staff.

In fairness to the Committee, Bill Ray's requests were denied or radically scaled down by the commissioners and the Bureau of the Budget before they got to Congress. But had the Committee insisted he be given more investigators he might have received them.

The Committee insisted the Commission undertake a study of the power of conglomerate corporations in broadcasting, offering a million dollars for the task. The Commission balked, ultimately undertook a very modest look at the problem, killed the project, and took no action.

At one time the Commission abandoned an investigation of AT&T's rates because it didn't have enough auditors. The Defense Department's Defense Communications Agency, itself a major customer of Bell, said it had 3,000 auditors available and would gladly loan the Commission what it needed. The commissioners, red-faced, realizing their bluff had been called, delayed until Defense Secretary Mel Laird could countermand the offer.

The Committee did take an interest in increasing the Commission's Common Carrier Bureau staff, though it has never been given even a small portion of the resources it would need to adequately regulate the $50-billion Bell.

The substantive committees (the Communications Subcommittees of the House Interstate and Foreign Commerce Committee and the Senate Commerce Committee) not only hold hearings on new legislation, but also hold oversight hearings from time to time. These tend to degenerate into the FCC Chair's reading a long, self-serving statement describing the great job he has been doing, and House members or senators either not attending or walking in and out and asking questions for the industry or their constituents (*e.g.*, why their good friends couldn't get licenses to operate radios in their power boats and private planes in something under 60 days). Such hearings offer a tremendous opportunity for public-spirited legislators to demand a better performance from the commissioners, and they have occasionally risen to the responsibility.

The House Committee also had an Investigations Subcommittee which uncovered the scandals at the FCC in the 1950s. It would probe around into especially egregious cases and outlandish instances of commissioner behavior (such as Chairman Dean Burch wiretapping one of his own employees). The Senate Committee never mustered such curiosity about the FCC, perhaps because at least one House investigation (the WIFE case) led to charges of untoward influence and participation by a Senate Committee staff member.

Finally, senators and congressmen can call and write FCC commissioners and staff. The Commission can resist such inquiries when it wishes. It took the agency 18 months to provide a report of who owned the nation's broadcast stations to an inquiring senator. That was not entirely a matter of agency intransigence. The Commission's records were in a horrible state of disarray and it had never before organized them for its own use. As it turned out, even after this lengthy preparation, the Senator was later able to point out numerous errors in the FCC's report.

But there is nevertheless such a mystical aura about congressional mail (it is generally given a pink cover slip) that it receives relatively prompt handling and is often the subject of discussion at Commission meetings.

When you consider these activities together – appointments, legislation, appropriations, oversight, investigations, personal inquiries – clearly Congress holds tremendous potential power for good or ill over the regulatory commissions.

But how is that power likely to be used? Let us assume for a moment the highest of motives on the part of our elected officials, or at worst their neutrality. The result of their processing the enormous flow of paper, mail, phone messages, and visitors through their offices is that they end up using almost all their time and power for little save industry representation. Industry lobbyists are the ones who have the greatest incentive to press their views upon the legislators and their staff assistants. Consumers tend to be uninformed, unorganized, and unheard. If one assumes large campaign contributions are also involved, or the official considers citizens as troublemakers, the scales are even more heavily tipped for the special interests.

There is no easy way to turn this situation around. Industry representatives have a right to be heard. They will almost always be able to field the heaviest linemen and the fastest backs. But there is no reason to give them a clear field in which to run wild.

Aside from individual citizens monitoring their own congressmen and senators, the most obvious way to deal with the problem is some form of citizens' lobby representing the public's interest on broadcasting issues. It would take an army of lobbyists, backed up by a million-member citizens' organization, to really do battle with the broadcasters, and there is no way to organize and fund such an operation. But even one or two people on the Hill can have an amazing impact. They may not win every game, but at least scores of 35-7 are better than 99-0. And occasionally – based on the few experiments that have been tried – they can even win.

Media. What about the press? There are many mutually reinforcing reasons for the inadequate reporting of the regulatory commissions. It is not unfair to observe that those who would suffer most from such stories are the same corporations that provide the lion's share of the media's advertising revenue. Dirty politics is fair journalistic game; exposing it may even be good politics. White collar crime and unethical corporate practices are another matter.

What a dramatic example Watergate provided! There were relatively thorough, for Congress, investigations of the relevant political figures by the Senate and House committees. Although the media largely ignored George McGovern's charges in 1972, once President Nixon was safely reelected and the unraveling of Watergate showed it to be one of the largest political scandals in our nation's history, the sparrows of the Washington press corps flew into it like an open granary.

But the large corporations and the rich who had paid for it all with their tens of millions of dollars in political contributions – in return for which they continue to reap the largest returns ever offered the American investor – were virtually ignored. The Senate's Watergate hearings sort of fizzled out once the senators had no witnesses left save respectable corporate executives, many of whom were also among their major donors. And the media seemed to find the crimes of their advertisers less newsworthy than the crimes of elected officials.

But it is both unfair and simplistic to suggest this is the only reason for the failure to report federal regulatory commissions' scandals.

It is unfair because there is probably no reputable news gathering organization in the country that has not on some occasion reported stories adversely affecting its advertisers. It does, however, take a little added courage and incentive to uncover and carry such a story, and if there are any legitimate reasons for avoiding the story it is easiest to let it go by the board.

It is too simplistic because there are a great number of other reasons.

Regulatory commission stories are perceived by reporter and audience alike as dull and complicated. The FCC and its sister commissions are notoriously obtuse in explaining their actions. The subgovernments of Washington cloud unlimited discretion and personal favoritism in a gobbledygook that convinces themselves, and long ago frightened everyone else into the insecurity of believing, that expertise is somehow involved. A reporter with no hesitancy in reporting the intricacies of cost overruns on ABM missiles doubts his or her ability to comprehend an FCC commissioners' decision to award the Bell Telephone Company a $1 billion rate increase which the FCC staff and hearing examiner found to be unwarranted.

It is very expensive to cover an agency. The trade press does it. *Broadcasting* magazine will assign one or more reporters to cover the FCC. But there are, at most, a half-dozen other agencies in Washington of interest to the magazine's readers. By contrast, the *Washington Post* has hundreds of agencies it could monitor, and ideally should. A general newspaper has neither the space nor enough interested readers to warrant the kind of detailed reporting about an agency's doings that fills the pages of *Broadcasting*. The kind of long news or feature pieces it can use take a lot of time to develop. A reporter capable of turning out three relatively easy stories in a day may need six weeks or more to discover, understand, investigate and write an expose about the FCC.

It takes first class investigative reporters to dig stories out of the regulatory commissions. There are no more than a handful in Washington, and they are so overworked as to threaten their health and marriages. It doesn't always produce a story. When it does there's little glory, except for the reporters who break a Watergate story. Given the choice between the glitter and glamour of the White House press corps and the dusty grey walls of a regulatory commission it takes a committed journalist to choose the latter. It's less stressful to copy down what the Secretary of Defense says at his morning press conference, write it up, file it, and go home to an early dinner than to be wading through agency files and tracking down 100 leads into all hours of the night.

The fact remains that a quarter to a third of our gross national product, as well as the nation's stock markets and banks, are subject to the control of regulatory commissions. These are the agencies that discourage or accelerate inflation, determine the quality of the food and drugs we consume, the future of our passenger railroad system and the radio and television programs we watch. The lives of millions of Americans are being affected in dozens of ways by regulatory commission decisions that go unreported or inadequately analyzed by the media.

As a result, commissioners are sitting on regulatory commissions who have either a negative or neutral influence; big business dominates the proceedings in ways that are at least undesirable and occasionally illegal; decisions are announced with opinions so obtuse or vacuous as to be laughable, and the American public continues to suffer in ignorance.

Most responsible news gathering organizations are conscious of their failing in this regard and have tried various schemes for rectifying it. I know of no substitute for taking one reporter and giving him or her a top priority assignment of covering one agency for no less than a year or two.

The stories should be run as national news rather than, or in addition to, the business page stories.

There are a number of large news gathering operations in Washington: *New York Times*, *Washington Post*, *Wall Street Journal*, Associated Press, United Press International, *Time* magazine, *Newsweek*, three TV networks, and more. Each has a large enough staff that at least one reporter could be assigned to a regulatory commission. Other smaller but top-quality Washington news bureaus, like those of the

Los Angeles Times or *Des Moines Register*, might also want to participate.

Once a story has been broken by one of them, others would come to cover it as they would any other major Washington news. If such organizations could spread their reporters around and cover in total, say, a dozen agencies for two years, the impact upon American journalism, consumers, Congress, and the regulatory commissions would be enormous. If this proposal won't work for some reason, let them come up with something that will. But the failure to cover the daily work, and even the scandals in our regulatory commissions has now become a scandal itself to which the press simply must respond.

Universities and foundations. Throughout my years on the Commission I made enormous efforts to encourage foundations, research think tanks and academic institutions to concern themselves with research, analysis, teaching and writing about communications policies in general and broadcasting in particular. Some came to see the wisdom and need for such undertakings on their own at about the same time. There has been an increased commitment, and much of the work has been first-rate. By no means do I mean to slight this crucial element of reform.

Many research and academic institutions are frightened, ill equipped, or precluded by law from engaging in action or applied research. Such institutions are often well staffed and funded by government, foundations, industry grants, and wealthy philanthropists. In fact, person-for-person and dollar-for-dollar there are far more resources for research than for the lobbying and litigation necessary to turn that research into action affecting industry decisions and government policy making. Academics' fear that they might lose funding if they were to work for the change suggested by their research, especially if it would displease donors, which is as understandable as it is unfortunate.

What you can do. Are you interested in helping with these challenges? Do you have a choice of where to contribute your money or time? If so, because of the restraints on some research and academic programs, I would counsel you to contribute your talents to action-oriented organizations and programs. It will give you a proportionately much greater impact.

Similarly, my own instincts as an academic are that greater learning opportunities are presented, and more imagination and enthusiasm brought to the task, when students can experience the impact of their learning, research, writing and advocacy on the real world. The academic quality of such projects is generally superior, in my experience, to that of more theoretical studies.

There are generally dozens of rulemakings pending at the FCC. Many will not be ripe for decision for a year or eighteen months. Effort put into a study of the issues raised by a given rulemaking can produce a document filed with the Commission. Don't be discouraged if your brilliant public interest analysis is not immediately enacted by the FCC. But know that you've had more impact than if you had published it in an obscure academic journal that few subscribe to and fewer still read. On the other hand, know that an equivalent amount of effort invested in FCC actions to be decided next week, or were disposed of last year, will have little or no impact. A simple inquiry regarding a rulemaking's status can make all the difference.

Or suppose you're interested in monitoring the performance of your local radio and television stations or examining their logs and public files. Terrific. It's always a worthwhile undertaking. Better still, involve a high school or college class, members of a union local, church, or community group in the process.

As long as you're doing it, why not look forward to the next license renewal cycle in your area? See if there are local groups interested in challenging licenses, put your data in a form that can make a difference, and announce it to your community in a major press conference or assembly. It will take little additional effort. Even if the station's license is renewed you may succeed in significantly altering the station's performance.

Maybe you're outraged by a program or commercial practice. Write your local station, sponsor, elected officials and the FCC? Sure. But as long as you're at it, why not write your letter in the form of a petition to the FCC, circulate it among a dozen or more local groups in your area for their support and signature, send a delegation to your local general manager to present it in person as a community-wide venture, and multiply your effectiveness a hundred fold for very little additional effort.

Get the idea? Facts are essential. Just shooting off your mouth will accomplish little and may not even make you feel better. But fact-gathering and report-writing taken alone will have little more effect. Knowing a little bit about your legal rights, associating with others in support of your cause, picking the right time, form and procedure for your report can be a lot more fun and effective.

Don't underestimate what your own modest philanthropy can accomplish. Even one percent of your income can make a difference to the little, public interest activities you choose to support. Many public interest lawyers who could earn three times as much are working for $5,000 or $10,000 a year. Many organizations operate on budgets of under $25,000 a year. A year's effort from a talented and dedicated young person can work wonders in Washington, or elsewhere. Participating in government proceedings or filing lawsuits against large corporations can improve the quality of our lives, including our television. Occasionally it can have a multi-million-dollar impact. Fifty people contributing $100 each can support such a public interest lawyer. That's not a lot of people or money. But it can make a lot of difference. If they only give $10 each that's also significant. You just need a few more people to raise the money. Choose your organizations carefully, but then support them generously. Your contribution to a $300 billion federal budget may go unnoticed. Your contribution to a $5,000 public interest lawyer won't.

The fact is you **can** make a difference. As Margaret Mead reminded us, "Never doubt that a small group of thoughtful, committed, citizens can change the world. Indeed, it is the only thing that ever has."

Teacher or student, community leader or

housewife, elected official or consumer, journalist or newspaper reader, each of us can have an impact on the performance of radio and television in this country. Channeling our outrage into public interest law firms, community media reform organizations, national lobbying efforts, and the most effective individual citizen's actions will have that impact. All of us, even the broadcasters, will be the better for it.

###

About the Author

Nicholas Johnson was born and raised in Iowa City, Iowa (1934-1952). He holds undergraduate and law degrees from the University of Texas, Austin. Following graduation, he clerked for U.S. Fifth Circuit Court of Appeals Judge John R. Brown and U.S. Supreme Court Justice Hugo L. Black. After teaching at the University of California, Berkeley, law school and practicing with Covington & Burling, Washington, President Lyndon Johnson appointed him U.S. Maritime Administrator. He is best known for his tumultuous seven-year term as a commissioner of the Federal Communications Commission. Until his retirement (2014) he was teaching at the University of Iowa College of Law, having returned from Washington to his hometown in 1980 and boyhood family house in 1989. He has travelled widely and played a variety of roles: congressional primary candidate and school board member; author, columnist, and public lecturer; corporate lawyer and public interest advocate; TV host and radio commentator; and a public health policy institute co-director. In 2009 he was included in *The Yale Biographical Dictionary of American Law* as one of 700 individuals described by the publisher as "leading figures in the history of American law, from the colonial era to the present day." Website and contact information: https://www.nicholasjohnson.org. Blog: https://FromDC2Iowa.blogspot.com.

Acknowledgements

The accomplishments during my terms as Administrator, Maritime Administration (MARAD), 1964-1966, and Commissioner, Federal Communications Commission (FCC), 1966-1973, would not have been possible without the contributions of a bright and able team of young friends: my staff, legal assistants and over 100 interns and seminar students. They have my deep appreciation and affection for their exceptional ability and good cheer.

MARAD. My personal MARAD staff included Stephen J. Friedman, Margaret Saywell, Robert Thorpe and Mary Ann Bittel Tsucalas.

FCC. The FCC staff included Doris Coles, Bonnie Herbert, Robert Thorpe, and Mary Ann Tsucallas. Those who served as legal assistants were Robert Bennett, Richard Brodsky, John Jay Dystel, Jeffrey R. Freund, Larry Gage, Gary G. Gerlach, James Hoak, Tom Jones, Jr., Simon Lazarus III, and Tracy Westen.

Most all, including interns, have gone on to remarkable careers in education, government, business, law and life. Indeed, the only reason all interns and students are not listed here is because, by 2019, records for most of them are missing or incomplete. It seemed unkind and unwise to mention some and leave others to wonder why they were not included. If it ever becomes possible to list all of them, they may be included in future editions.

Cover Photo Credits

Index